Magical Mind Gardens

Books by Gloria Chadwick

*Discovering Your Past Lives: The Ultimate
Guide Into and Through Your Past Life Memories*

Travel through time to explore everything you want
to know about your past lives and balance your karma.

*The Complete Do-it-Yourself Guide to Past Life
Regression: Time Tripping Adventures Into Your Soul*

Offers everything you need to know and more
about traveling into and through your past lives.

Looking Into Your Future Lives: A Trip Through Time

Travel through multidimensional vibrations of time into and
through the realms and realities your soul has experienced.

*Magical Mind, Magical Life: How to Live a
Magical Life, Filled with Happiness and Light*

Your mind is magical. You are magical. You
hold the key to a magical life within your mind.

*Whispers Beyond the Rainbow:
A Soul's Journey Into Awakening*

A magical rainbow journey inspires you
on a quest to awaken your spiritual self.

*Magical Mind Gardens: Grow Your Mind Into
a Beautiful Garden of Harmony and Joy*

Your mind is a fertile garden that will
grow whatever thoughts you plant.

Inner Journeys: Meditations and Guided Visualizations

Guided visualizations can take you on many wonderful inner journeys
that lead you into the multidimensional worlds of your mind and soul.

Somewhere Over the Rainbow: A Soul's Journey Home

A visionary novel about the reality of reincarnation
that offers a lighthearted look into the ups and
downs of being spiritual in a physical world.

Magical Mind Gardens

*Grow Your Mind Into a Beautiful
Garden of Harmony and Joy*

Gloria Chadwick

Light Library

Magical Mind Gardens

Grow Your Mind Into a Beautiful Garden of Harmony and Joy

Echoes of Mind ~ Book Two

© 2022 by Gloria Chadwick

All rights reserved. No part of this book may be reproduced or utilized in any form or by any means without permission in writing from the publisher, except for brief quotations used in a review.

Publisher's Cataloging-in-Publication Data

Amberson, Renee / Chadwick, Gloria

Magical Mind Gardens

1. Positive Mind Power 2. Self-Help 3. Happiness
4. Personal Growth / Transformation I. Title

ISBN 10: 1-883717-29-9
ISBN 13: 978-1-883717-29-2

Light Library
https://lightlibrary.blogspot.com

This book is dedicated to Magi… the light of my life who brings me joy and happiness in every moment.

Contents

Introduction 11
Invites you to look within your mind to see the magical power you have in growing joy and happiness in your life.

January ~ New Beginnings 15
Your mind is magical. You are magical. The power of your mind is totally awesome. You have the ability to create a magical life simply by the thoughts you hold in your mind.

February ~ Love and Happiness 27
You can be happy and follow your bliss. You can bring joy and light into your life. You can let love shine in all your experiences.

March ~ Growing Your "Self" 37
You can grow yourself into the magical person you truly are.

April ~ Nature of Harmony 49
Everything in nature is in balance and harmony with itself. Everything in your mind—in your thoughts and feelings—is in harmony with everything you experience.

Garden of Harmony 59
Be in a beautiful garden filled with lush, green plants and flowers that vibrate with health and harmony.

May ~ Imagination and Intuition 65
    Look into your imagination to see your intuition and insights, and to recognize the inner knowing you have within you. Play with your thoughts and watch them grow into your experiences.

June ~ Seeding Your Subconscious 75
    The power of words and what your words can do for you. Words are magical. Words have power. Words can change any feeling or experience.

July ~ Freedom ~ Letting Go 87
    Allow yourself to be free, to let go of anything that might be holding you back. Let yourself go with the flow, and explore wonderful new possibilities.

August ~ Perspectives and Perceptions 97
    Seeing and reading the signs from your inner self and your magical mind. Changing the way you look at things.

September ~ Creating Your Reality 109
    You create everything you experience in your life through your thoughts and feelings.

October ~ Choices and Changes 121
    Lighten up. Look at the bright side. Change your mind. It may change your life.

November ~ Gratitude 133
    Being thankful for everything in your life also means being thankful for what is coming into your life and recognizing the many blessings you already have.

December ~ Giving and Receiving 143
    You can have everything you want. The Universe wants you to have everything you want.

About the Author

Your subconscious mind is a beautiful garden, waiting to grow whatever thoughts you plant.

Introduction

Gardens are peaceful, pleasant, inspiring places where beauty, harmony, and serenity abound. Gardens are a pleasure to experience and you can grow whatever you want in the gardens of your own mind. Whenever you think, you open and enter the garden of your mind.

Magical Mind Gardens invites you to look within your mind to see the magical power you have in growing joy and happiness in your life. It grew out of **Magical Mind, Magical Life**, which is about living a magical life by opening the magic inside your mind.

The key to living a magical life, filled with happiness and light, is a positive attitude. By clearing out the negatives and looking at the sunny side of things, you automatically bring happiness and harmony into your life.

This book picks up where *Magical Mind* leaves off; it offers you 365 ways to make your life more special and magical, meaningful in every way, filled with wonder and joy, harmony and light. It offers you magical thoughts you might want to plant in your mind, as well as a very special Garden of Harmony meditation, excerpted from *Magical Mind, Magical Life*.

Since there are 365 magical thoughts (with an extra one thrown in just in case it's a leap year when you're reading this book), I hope you'll take your time, reading one thought a day and thinking about it for a while. Ponder it. Meditate on it. Let it gently swirl through your mind and see what thoughts and feelings come to you. Or you might want to open the book at random and read the magical thought on any page.

Let it be a process that shows you the magic you have inside your mind as you plant magical mind gardens. These magical thoughts are merely suggestions you might want to incorporate into your life if they feel right for you. There are also a lot of things you might want to think about as you create the reality you experience every day.

In many ways the magical thoughts inside this book are really little reminders of what you already know and do on a daily basis. I hope you'll find the magical thoughts uplifting and powerful, and that they will serve as a guide for helping you remember what you already know.

Imagination is how you work in your mind garden. Your thoughts are how you tend your garden. Imagining means to hold a mental picture of something that is not physically present. Using the seeds of imagination, you can grow beautiful, wonderful, amazing experiences that begin in your magical mind garden.

January

New Beginnings

January

New Beginnings

January 1—**Mind Gardens**

Imagine a beautiful mind garden…

Imagine your subconscious mind is a beautiful, fertile garden that will grow whatever thoughts and feelings you plant.

What you plant and cultivate in your mind's garden grows into what you experience. What you hold in your thoughts and feelings becomes a reality in your life.

Plant positive thoughts and watch them grow. As you plant positive seeds in your mind, be sure to lavish them with an abundance of positive attention and shower them with light. Nurture your thoughts and feelings with care as you nourish the growing magic inside your mind. Tend your garden every day with loving care and attention.

Grow some beautiful thoughts. Grow your mind into a magical garden—a place of harmony, joy, and light—filled with positive thoughts and happy feelings, and watch them grow.

January 2—**Something Special is Happening**

Something very special and magical is going to happen for you today. Expect it. Know that it's going to happen. Eagerly anticipate it with happiness, joy, and excitement. Really feel it in your heart, mind, and soul. Be open to receiving it, accepting it, and enjoying it.

Living every day of your life in hopeful anticipation of wonderful things happening is a joyful, happy way to live.

By actually expecting wonderful things or absolutely knowing that whatever is happening in your life is truly wonderful will cause and create your life to be filled with wonderful things.

January 3—*Love What You Do; Do What You Love*

Loving what you do and doing what you love will bring forth joy and happiness within you. The vibration of loving... no matter what it is, elevates your energies to the highest level.

If you're not loving what you do, then find something—anything—in what you do that brings you joy and focus on that. By focusing on what brings you joy, you will find—to your absolute delight—that you will truly begin to love what you do.

By loving—even a little bit—what you do, you will create a space—a pathway—to move forward toward more joy and happiness.

January 4—*Clearing the Clutter*

Let go of all the "stuff" that no longer serves you. The stuff that may be holding you back. Toss the trash from your mind and drop the heavy baggage that weighs you down. Create a clear space to move forward and welcome new experiences into your life.

As you clear out the clutter in your life, you may find a few very nice surprises—perhaps treasures you've buried a long time ago and have forgotten. Looking at them, deciding whether to keep them or throw them away, you realize how valuable and precious some of these things are now, and how they offer you wonderful new opportunities. Incorporate these wonderful things into your life.

January 5—*A Magical Mindset*

Create a magical mindset, a place inside your mind where your thoughts and ideas can be nourished and grow. A magical mindset is a frame of mind that allows wonderful, beautiful thoughts and ideas to flourish, in a positive atmosphere of acceptance.

January 6—*Wish List*

Wishes are filled with magic and power. Make a wish list. A wish list is things you don't have that you wish you had. A wish list contains anything you want, whether it seems possible or impossible.

List a few things you wish for right now. Think about all the wonderful things you'd like to have and what you would do with them if you had them.

Look through your wish list. What is your dearest wish? Look inside your heart for your most treasured hope or desire.

Think about it for a few minutes, then go inside your imagination and wish it into existence with your inner power. Believe it with all your heart, mind, and soul, and your wish will come true.

You don't have to know how your wish will come about; you just have to *believe* that it will happen.

If your belief is true, things will happen to make your wish come true. Situations and circumstances will come into your life, people will help you through casual comments, things you read will inspire you or give you direction, and a multitude of chances, coincidences, and synchronicities will occur.

You know, in a magical place inside your mind, that your wish is already on its way to becoming true, to being real in your physical world.

Do one thing—big or small—today to bring your wish into your life. While wishing will make it happen, acting on it will make it happen even faster. Put the energy of your wish into motion.

January 7—*Purely Positive*

Positive energy behind a positive thought always brings a positive result.

January 8—*Powerful Possibilities*

Open yourself up to new possibilities.

You feel a sense of power building up inside you as you realize that whatever you want to achieve is entirely possible. In fact, you have a strong sense that it's really going to happen.

You know it. You can feel it inside you. There's a flutter of joy and happiness in your heart, a knowing, that wasn't there before. A flutter of energy and anticipation flows through you.

January 9—*Commitment*

Make a commitment to do something—a sacred promise to yourself. Then follow through.

January 10—*Hello, It's Me*

Hi. This is your inner self. I've been trying to reach you for a while. I know you're busy with work and relationships, and day-to-day stuff, but I'd really like to talk to you.

I hang out in your subconscious mind. Come find me. Let's be friends. We need to talk. I'm here, whenever you need me.

January 11—*Leaning*

Look at what you're leaning toward doing to lead you in the right direction. Whatever you're leaning toward, you're also being pulled or drawn into by your inner self and/or the Universe.

January 12—*A Brilliant Idea*

A wonderful, absolutely brilliant idea just popped into your mind. Maybe it's been there for a while, budding just below the surface, waiting for you to recognize it.

When you become aware of it, you probably think to yourself, "That's Brilliant!" You can't help but not think that. This is also known as an *aha moment*, when everything falls into place perfectly. It may come into your mind after you've been pondering something for a while.

When it appears, be sure to acknowledge your brilliant idea. In fact, it's hard not to acknowledge it because it's so brilliant and fills you with hope and joy and purpose.

January 13—**Think About It**

Think about what you want to do, what you want to achieve. Think about how you'll go about incorporating this thing you want to do into your life. Think about what you need to do to make this thing happen.

Then put your thoughts into motion and make it happen.

January 14—**Reminders**

Remind yourself every day that you are a magical, powerful person. Remind yourself that you have the ability to create what you want—whenever you want.

January 15—**What's on Your Mind?**

What are you thinking about right this minute? What's on your mind? Spend some time with the thought you have in your mind right now to see what's on your mind.

January 16—**Picture Perfect**

Look at everything you see today as totally perfect, beautiful in every way. If you see something you think isn't absolutely perfect, then picture it as perfect in your mind.

Because you see something as perfect, it *is* perfect, and you can allow it to become even more perfect. You're manifesting perfection from a magical point of view. Everything is already perfect. You just need to see it the way it really is—perfect in every aspect.

What you may have previously thought of as not perfect—perhaps a failed relationship, loss of a friendship, or maybe a job opportunity that didn't happen—are actually perfect because you see the perfection in the experience, you gain all the good from the situation, and you realize that they ARE actually perfect.

January 17—*Looking Forward*

Do you wake up each morning looking forward to what this wonderful new day will bring? Do you look forward to doing whatever it is that you'll be doing later today?

January 18—*Baby Steps*

If you're beginning a new project or creating something entirely new for yourself, take baby steps. While it's important to see the big picture, it's also important to see how you're going to get there.

One step at a time will get you where you want to go.

January 19—*What's Going to Happen?*

No one knows for sure what is going to happen or exactly how it's going to happen. That's what makes the journey toward getting what you want so fun and exciting.

You may not know where you're going or how to get there, but you are going to get there. Things will happen along the way, new ideas and insights will present themselves to you.

Every day is filled with fun surprises and unexpected happy occurrences you experience along the way as you travel the path toward the new reality you're beginning to create for yourself, and before you know it, you've arrived at where you wanted to go.

January 20—*Fresh Start*

Give yourself a fresh start, a new beginning. Acknowledge what has happened in the past, then let go of the old and bring in the new. Every day offers you wonderful opportunities to start anew, to begin a fresh approach.

January 21—*Set Yourself Up to Succeed*

Your thoughts, feelings, and actions will determine whether you succeed or fail. Set yourself up for success by holding the thought of success in your mind. Focus your actions and energies toward success—whatever that means to you.

See yourself succeeding in what you want to achieve. Feel yourself succeeding. See yourself in the picture of what success means to you. Feed success with positive thoughts which will generate the energy and power for your thought to succeed.

January 22—*Glimmers*

You saw that, didn't you? That glimmer inside your mind that just appeared out of nowhere and for no reason that filled you with pure joy and happiness? I know you felt it, even if you didn't see it.

That's your inner self, saying, "Hi" to you, shimmering inside your mind—just waiting to show you all the magic within yourself.

January 23—*No Way! Yes, Way!*

If you think there's really no way something can happen, you might want to think again.

There is always a way to make something happen, to look at something in a new way. It begins with you knowing that yes, there is a way.

January 24—*Take Care of Your Thoughts*

Watch your thoughts. They happen.

Be careful what you wish for. You might just get it.

Be even more careful what you think about. It will happen.

Choose the good thoughts—the kind, loving thoughts—the ones that feel happy and joyful—the ones your inner self whispers to you that are always in your magical mind.

Take care to think only good thoughts

January 25—*It's a Possibility*

One of the first steps in creating the reality you want to experience is to really know that it is entirely possible.

Let the possibility play gently on your mind a bit; ponder it for a while before you begin to turn a possibility into a reality.

January 26—*Finding Hidden Treasure*

Do you ever wish you could find a hidden treasure and become rich? Would you believe me if I told you that you have always had access to this wonderful hidden treasure in your mind simply by engaging the magical power you have within you?

It's true. The hidden treasure is really your hidden potential to create everything you want—and to live in abundance, in every part of your life—by using the magical power of your mind. The only reason it's hidden is because you haven't fully recognized it yet and put it into motion.

Looking for hidden treasure? Look within. Remember what you've always known: You create what you experience through your thoughts and feelings. Focus the power of your mind toward what you want and put your positive energy into action.

January 27—*Sketches*

When an artist begins to paint a masterpiece picture, he starts by sketching a silhouette, a framework by which to fill in the details of the picture—the shape of things to come.

When a writer begins to write a book, she sketches out the structure—the form and shape of what's going inside the book, creating an outline to fill in the pages with words.

You are an artist—you paint the pictures of your life. You are a writer—you write the experiences in your life.

Begin to create the reality you want to live by first creating the structure, the framework, the silhouette, and the outline of what you want in your life. Begin to create the shape of things to come.

Fill in the details along the way on your journey to creating the life you want to live.

January 28—*Make a Motto*

Make a motto—a credo—to live by. A motto that reflects who you are and the attitude you hold toward all things in your life.

A motto is a sentence or two that captures the entirety of your attitude and outlook on life.

Make a motto that fits your lifestyle and your view of life that is in harmony with who you are. Then, live by that motto.

January 29—*The Right Wavelength*

When you tune into the right frequency—the energies that are right for you—everything comes to you naturally and easily—just like magic—seemingly without any effort on your part.

Being on the right wavelength is being in the flow of good energy. Find your frequency and tune into it. There are many ways to make this happen, and being positive is probably the best way to tune into the right wavelength for you.

Let yourself get into the flow of everything good, and the right wavelength will tune into you.

January 30—*Joyful Journeys*

All of life is a journey. Every day is a wonderful new adventure. It's not so much reaching the destination at the end of a journey as it is the journey to arrive there—the steps and experiences you have along the way.

The joy is in the journey; every step offers lessons to help you learn and gifts for you to enjoy. Travel lightly on your path, experiencing joy and happiness in all your experiences.

January 31—*You are Always Magical*

Your mind is magical. You are magical. The power of your mind is totally awesome.

Believe in the magical power of your mind and your magical ability to create whatever you want, whenever you want, simply by the thoughts you hold in your mind.

You are always magical.

February

Love and Happiness

February

―――――――――― ∽ ――――――――――

Love and Happiness

February 1—*Just be Happy*

One of the most powerful, positive things you can do is to *just be happy*. Give yourself permission to just be happy, no matter what is happening in your life. Happiness comes from within and is always available to you. Feel the joy of happiness in your heart.

Happiness is a wonderful gift you give yourself. Think happy. Be happy. Send happy thoughts to yourself every day, all day, all the time. Smile and just be happy.

February 2—*Good Vibes*

Your words, thoughts, and feelings are made of energy. This energy can be either positive or negative, depending on what you say, think, and feel.

Send yourself some good vibrations. Say nice things, think positive thoughts, and feel the energy of love and happiness in your magical mind.

February 3—*Happy Dance*

Today, when no one is looking, do a happy dance. Be wild and carefree, exuberant and joyful.

February 4—*Open Your Heart*

Open your heart to let love in. Open yourself to receiving love from many sources.

Keep an open heart and love will flow to you.

February 5—*Hinges*

What sort of "hinges" do you have in your life?

Do you ever say to yourself, "I'll be happy if... I get a better job, a new relationship, if a certain thing works out for me, if only such and such would happen, or whatever."

Does your happiness hinge on things outside of yourself?

February 6—*I Love You*

Tell someone—a person or a pet—how much you love them. Really feel the love you have for this person or pet deep inside you. Let it well up within you until it fills your entire heart.

February 7—*Choose Happiness*

Every day, in every moment, in every experience, in every situation, you have a choice. Choose the things that make you happy. Choose happiness.

February 8—*Follow Your Bliss*

You can be happy and follow your bliss. You can bring joy and light into your life. You can let love shine in all your experiences. It's as easy as simply deciding to follow your bliss.

February 9—*Smile*

Smile for no reason at all. If you need a reason, then smile because it makes you happy. Smile just for the sake of smiling.

The simple act of smiling lifts you up and fills you with happiness. Notice how much lighter you feel.

February 10—**Reminders**

Remind yourself every day that you are a wonderful, special, powerful, magical person.

It's true. You really are all that and so much more. Remind yourself of that.

February 11—**Give Yourself Permission**

Let yourself be who you truly are. Let yourself live and breathe, and sing and dance. Let yourself live the life you want to live. Let go of anything that is holding you back from being truly happy.

Thank it for being in your life, forgive it if you need to, bless it, and let it go. Just let it go and give yourself permission to grow.

February 12—**Just Because**

Do something today just because you want to. Do something just because it makes you happy.

February 13—**Lighten Up**

Don't take yourself too seriously. Sometimes the Universe—in the process of giving you what you want—will show you things or cause events to occur in a light-hearted manner to get you back on track and guide you in the right direction.

It usually happens when you take yourself and what you are creating way too seriously, and you're bound and determined to create the reality you want, and you feel as if you're going to create it and make it happen, no matter what.

Creating your reality is supposed to be fun and easy, not hard work, and the Universe—with its wonderful sense of humor—occasionally needs to remind you of that by showing you a joke or helping you to see the humor in something you are doing to make you laugh at yourself and lighten up.

Look at it as an inside joke. When you get the joke, and the funny in it, and laugh about it, you realize that the Universe is totally guiding you in the right direction.

February 14—*You are Loved*

Feel totally, completely, unconditionally loved. Let this feeling fill you until you are overflowing with it, until your heart is completely filled with the joy and happiness and feeling of love.

Feel it circulating within and through you, opening your heart, freeing you from any and all past hurts, letting them go in an easy, carefree, loving manner.

Feel this love permeating every part of your life. Feel it surrounding you in every thought, word, and emotion you have; feel it in every situation, in every relationship, and in every experience. See everything totally filled with love and surrounded by love.

February 15—*More, Please*

There's more than enough love to go around. There is an infinite, ever-growing, always-abundant source of love that is always there. Serve up second helpings of happiness and love. Lots and lots of second helpings.

February 16—*What Makes You Happy?*

Really think about this. What makes you happy? Why does it make you happy? How can you make more happiness in your life?

February 17—*Making Positive Changes*

Begin with who you are right now, and where you are in your life. See what is happening and what is around you—what you have to work with.

Look for all the good in what is in your life right now and go from there. Start from a positive place and let this be your springboard into making positive changes in your life.

February 18—*Joy and Laughter*

Put joy and laughter into your life on a daily basis.

It can work wonders.

February 19—*Embrace Yourself*

Everything you've ever experienced is part of you. All of it. Your past experiences have grown you into who you are now.

Embrace every part of yourself.

February 20—*Look for the Good*

There is good in everything. Good is everywhere, all the time, just waiting for you to see it and become aware of it.

Look for the good in all aspects of your life. It's always there.

February 21—*Look on the Bright Side*

Lighten up. Look at the bright side.

Change your mind. It may change your life.

February 22—*Smile at Yourself*

Look in the mirror and smile at yourself. Take the time to really appreciate something special about yourself.

It can be something you see on the outside or something you see on the inside. Notice how your smile lights up your eyes and your face.

February 23—*Telling Stories*

When you're alone with your thoughts, what do you tell yourself? What do your feelings say to you?

What images play in your mind? What stories does your subconscious tell you?

Listen to the stories you have running around in your mind to see if the stories are true—if they make you feel good about yourself or if they drag you down.

If you don't like the stories you tell yourself, rewrite them to tell you the true story.

February 24—*It's Such a Relief*

Let go of any burdens that weigh heavy on your mind. You'll feel so much lighter and happier when you let them go.

February 25—*Love Letter*

Write yourself a love letter, telling yourself how much you love yourself and why you love yourself.

February 26—*Are You in Love?*

Are you in love with all the people and situations in your life? Are you in love with everything you have?

Are you in love with everything that is happening in your life? Are you in love with the new reality you're creating for yourself? Are you in love with what you surround yourself with every day?

Are you in love with who you are? And who you are in the process of becoming?

Love is a very powerful energy. The more you love someone or something, the more it grows.

Be in love with everything in your life. If you're not in love with someone or something, let it go to make room for something else to come into your life that you can truly love.

February 27—*Wow! I Am Awesome!*

Take some time today, and every day, to recognize how awesome and truly magical you are. Really let this feeling fill you up completely. You are totally awesome!

February 28—*Toss the Trash*

Seriously, let go of all the trash in your life!! It's stinky and it doesn't belong in your life.

What does belong in your life are new, positive experiences that bring you happiness.

Toss the trash and let wonderful things begin to happen.

February 29—*Take the Leap*

If there's something you've been wanting to do, but are hesitant for any reason, today is the day to do it. Take a giant leap into your own power.

You have the power to change your life.

You have the magical power to change your mind and create a beautiful life, filled with happiness and light, simply by changing your mind. You can make your life everything you want it to be and more.

Take the leap.

March

Growing Your "Self"

March

Growing Your "Self"

March 1—**A Special Space**

Create a special place of harmony in your mind—a sacred sanctuary—that's all your own, where you can go to be peaceful and quiet within yourself, where the outside world can't intrude.

This is a special space where you can listen to your thoughts and feelings, and know what's truly going on beneath the surface, and how you really feel. It's a place where you can talk to your inner self to know your true feelings, where you can open your intuition and inner knowing.

Your sacred sanctuary is also a place of creation, where you can create the beginnings of everything you want in your life.

March 2—**Intuition**

When you just "know" something without knowing how you know, that's your intuition—your inner knowing—bubbling up and rising to the surface. Pay attention to those thoughts and feelings.

March 3—**Whispers**

Listen. Do you hear that? Someone whispering to you? A voice within trying to tell you something special, trying to be heard above the clamor of your conscious mind? Listen to the whispers of your inner self.

As you listen to the whispers, you'll discover and be able to clearly hear the voice of your inner self whispering to you in your heart and through your feelings, encouraging you to open the magic inside your mind.

March 4—*Dreaming*

Do you dream about doing something?
Or are you doing what you've dreamed about?

March 5—*Miracles in Motion*

You are perfect, just as you are. You're a unique, wonderful, magical person, special in every way. You are a miracle in motion.

See yourself as your inner self sees you to recognize the magic inside your mind. See yourself as the perfection-in-motion you truly are.

March 6—*Just Do It*

If you're a bit hesitant about doing something because you're not sure how it will turn out, but you really think you'd like to do it, then just do it! You may surprise yourself with what you can accomplish. Just do it. Do what's on your mind.

March 7—*Library of Knowledge*

Imagine you're in a library, filled with thousands of books that contain all the knowledge in the world and in the Universe. As you stand in the entrance to the library, you smell the rich scent of books and feel the essence of knowledge envelop you.

You know you're in a special, magical, sacred place. Walking into the library, you read some of the titles of the books. One book seems to call to you, and you feel magically drawn to it.

Walking over to the bookshelf, you reach for the book and read the title. Opening the book, you begin to read.

What is the title of the book, why were you drawn to it, and what knowledge does it give you?

March 8—*It's All About You*

Thinking about the library and some of the books you explored yesterday, and the knowledge you gained, you get a feeling that there is a very special, magical book that has your name on it.

Return to the library and read this very special book that's all about you.

March 9—*Growing Your Thoughts*

When you get an idea to do something that really appeals to you, feed that thought with energy and light. Let it grow into the beautiful experience it is destined to be.

March 10—*Challenge Yourself*

Challenge yourself to grow, to do whatever it takes to achieve what you want, especially if it seems far away and you're not sure what to do right now or how you can achieve it. **Believe** you can achieve it and work toward it every day in your thoughts, feelings, and most importantly—actions.

"I can do this!" With these words, and your positive attitude and actions, you will feel a power building inside you, helping you and enabling you to achieve your desired result.

Watch magical things begin to happen in your life as you grow toward your goal. Things will come into your life that align with your goal; new thoughts, ideas, and insights will sparkle into your mind, and pretty soon what you want to achieve—that may have seemed difficult at first—is what you'll begin to experience.

March 11—*What's Your Life Philosophy?*

A life philosophy is an over-arching view of how you see the events in your life and how you truly feel about things. Your life philosophy represents who you really are on the inside.

Your life philosophy was formed in your childhood and teenage years, based on what happened to you which caused you to see life in a particular manner. And life provided you with experiences that reinforced the beliefs you held.

Perhaps things happened that you had no control over and this caused you to believe you couldn't accomplish anything no matter how hard you tried, or perhaps you felt small and insignificant, and this caused you to believe that whatever you did was never good enough.

As you became an adult, that philosophy was firmly entrenched and embedded in your attitude about how you view life. You came to believe things that aren't really true. And this belief was reflected in your attitude, and in the things that now happen to you.

The good news is—if you don't like your life philosophy and it doesn't serve you well—you can change that philosophy; you can change the way you view life. You can create a new life philosophy that you really like—one that empowers you and reflects who you truly are—a magical person in every way.

March 12—*Qualities*

What do you like best about yourself? What is your best quality? Why is it your best quality?

It can be something about yourself on the inside that you admire or it can be something you see on the outside.

March 13—*What Can You Achieve?*

You know yourself better than anyone else. You know what you're capable of and how you can achieve what you want, based on your past experiences. You have a comfort zone.

What if you stepped out of your comfort zone? Maybe just a little? What if you walked away from your past patterns? Just let them go? What do you think would happen? What do you think you could achieve then?

Step out of your comfort zone and habitual patterns into new possibilities to see what you can achieve that is in line with the power you have to create what you want. Do things a little differently than you're used to doing and see what happens.

If you think you can achieve what you want, you can achieve it. Maybe it's time to step out of your comfort zone and re-arrange the way you do things.

March 14—*Take Care of Yourself*

Take the time, whenever you need it, to replenish and restore yourself—to shake off any bad vibes, and recharge your positive energies.

March 15—*Motivation*

What motivates you? Why do you want what you want? Look into your motivations to see where they're coming from.

Do you want to change something because you're experiencing negativity with it? If you come from a negative place in your mind to make changes, you probably won't like what you get. Negative begets negative.

Let yourself come from a good place to create what you want. Coming from a good place is very powerful in creating what you want to experience in your life. Change the negativity around first to understand why you want to make a change.

Look at how the negative situation has shown you positive things about yourself; maybe even shown you a new, positive course of direction to take, and how you can turn the situation around into a positive one.

This gives you the motivation and power to create what you want from there. Let yourself come from a good place to create even more good in your life.

March 16—*Growing*

Give yourself room to grow and leave lots of open spaces for unexpected and delightful surprises in the form of experiences and events, that you have no idea about now, to occur.

March 17—*Perish the Thought*

Whatever you worry about or fear, you will create an experience that reflects that worry or fear. You will cause and create it to be in your life. If you're holding any negative thoughts or feelings, it would be a really good idea to let them go. Perish those thoughts.

March 18—*Windows*

Open a window into new possibilities, into a new way of looking at things. Let the fresh, clean breeze from the open window clear out all the dust and cobwebs that may have accumulated.

March 19—*Be Nice to Yourself*

Take some time today to do something really nice for yourself. Show yourself how much you appreciate yourself.

March 20—*Work-in-Progress*

You are always in the process of being who you are and becoming who you want to be. You are an always-growing, ever-changing work-in-progress.

Enjoy the process of growing yourself every day—of growing the magic inside your mind.

See the progress you've already made in yourself—in growing your magical mind garden. Appreciate and congratulate yourself on what you've achieved so far, then keep on growing.

March 21—*Special Spring Morning*

The world is waking up from its winter's sleep, renewing and refreshing itself; coming alive, rebirthing itself. Breathe in the fresh, clean scent of the morning air and enjoy the feeling of being alive on such a beautiful, wondrous day.

Feel the gentle warmth of the sun on your face and skin. Feel the breeze as it softly caresses you. Notice the sparkling dewdrops on the early-morning green grass. See the early Spring flowers beginning to open up and bloom. Smell their beautiful fragrance. Notice their intricacy and detail, and the delicate profusion and variety of buds.

Notice how the buds are beginning to open up to the joyous light and the warmth of the sun. You feel the same way; you're opening up and growing into the magic inside your mind, seeing the seeds you've already planted begin to bloom and grow and blossom.

March 22—**Grow Yourself**

Grow yourself into the magical person you truly are. Fill your mind with positive thoughts, and watch them grow in your life— into wonderful experiences and a sense of happiness and joy that totally belongs to you.

March 23—**Connections**

Connect with your inner self—with the magical essence inside you. Take a few moments to be quiet, to listen to yourself.

Your inner self is your best friend, your confidant, your mentor—the one who will always give you the best advice and steer you in the right direction.

Your inner self has so many wonderful things to tell you, and is always up for helping you in whatever you want to do. Your inner self is your cheerleader, championing you onward and upward.

March 24—**Pursue Your Passion**

What are you passionate about? What brings you joy and happiness, and a sense of wonderful excitement?

What do you look forward to doing? What do you want to do more than anything else?

Pursue that passion.

March 25—**Say Nice Things**

I'm sure that when you were growing up, your mom told you, "If you can't say something nice, don't say anything at all." Moms are always so smart when it comes to these things.

When you feel hurt or angry, don't spout out these feelings. It's better to keep quiet and let these feelings go. If you say how you're feeling when you're in a negative frame of mind, you'll be sending out negative vibes which work like a boomerang and come back to bite you.

Say nice things whenever you can. And keep quiet when you can't.

March 26—*Take a "Me" Day*

Today is all about you, a day to just be who you are. You can do whatever you want—whatever makes you happy.

You can rest and recharge. You can be by yourself. You can surround yourself with the people you love. You can wear your favorite comfy clothes. You can sit in the sunshine. You can walk through the rain. You can simply be quiet with your thoughts. You can do whatever you want.

Whatever you want to do, today is a day to just be yourself.

March 27—*Pursuing Your Purpose*

Everyone needs a purpose in life; a reason to get out of bed in the morning. Without a purpose—something that gives meaning to your life—you may be wandering aimlessly around.

Find your purpose. You already know what it is. Then pursue it.

March 28—*Listen to Yourself*

If you're not sure about something, or don't know what your next step is, or how something will work out, talk to your inner self and listen to what your inner self tells you.

You may become aware of a new way to look at things or your inner self may offer you a sense of direction you weren't aware of before or hadn't even considered.

March 29—*Accomplishments*

Set a manageable, short-term goal; one you can accomplish today. Focus your full attention and awareness on it.

When you achieve it, be sure to congratulate yourself and notice how you feel. Accomplishing small goals sets you up to succeed for accomplishing big goals.

March 30—*Do Your Own Thing*

Follow your heart and do things the way *you* want to do them.

You're a unique person. Completely original and individual in every way. You know what works for you. Do things your own way. Create your own path; forge your own way ahead.

March 31—*It's a Surprise*

Your inner self is creating something very special and magical for you—a wonderful surprise. But you can't have it right now; you have to wait for it. Your inner self has just told you that it is coming your way, soon.

Let this happy thought brew in your mind. You know it's going to be something truly special. You feel it. You can't help smiling, wondering what it is. You feel a wonderful sense of anticipation building inside you, waiting to see what this wonderful surprise will be.

You know it's going to happen and you can hardly wait for it to appear so you can see what it is. You're so curious, wanting to know what it is. Perhaps you have a sense of what it is or an idea about what it might be. Your inner self may drop clues or give you hints of what is to come. On some level, you already know what it is. Take a guess.

What you may discover is that you've been creating this very wonderful surprise and keeping it secret so it can grow, in a pure and positive manner, and of its own accord. Whatever your inner self is creating for you, it will be something you're really going to like—a lot!

April

Nature of Harmony

April

Nature of Harmony

April 1—**Let it Grow**

Let an idea grow on you. Start with something small and watch it grow. It might be just a tiny thought to begin with, but the more you think about it, the more it appeals to you and grows on you.

April 2—**Stretch**

Everything in nature is in balance and harmony with itself. Everything in your mind—your thoughts and feelings—is in harmony with everything you experience in your life.

Grow your mind, grow your thoughts, grow your life into a beautiful place to be. Reach and stretch and grow into the magic and harmony and light that is within you.

April 3—**A Positive Outcome**

The nature of your subconscious mind is in harmony with all the thoughts and feelings you have. Your subconsciousness mind will always strive to be in harmony with the thoughts you have in your mind, and will always provide you with what you want, based on your thoughts and feelings. It's a big job, but your subconscious is up to it. It will make every thought you think and every feeling you feel happen—in one way or another.

The thoughts you hold and the feelings you have, and the picture you see in your mind of what you want is very, very powerful. No matter what you want to achieve, or what you want to have happen, always go about it in a positive way and envision a positive outcome.

April 4—*April Showers*

Remember when you were a child and you ran through the rain, loving the soft kisses of raindrops on your face and skin? Remember splashing in the mud puddles with carefree abandon and total joy?

Remember how you used to dance around in circles, your arms open wide to embrace the sky? Remember raising your face up and sticking out your tongue to catch the raindrops? Remember the sheer delight and pure happiness you felt inside you?

The next time it rains, run joyfully through the rain again. Take your shoes off and squish the mud between your toes. Splash in the puddles. Catch the raindrops on your tongue and taste their delicious wetness. Be totally happy that rain is falling in your life.

When the sun comes out, look up at the sky for a shimmering rainbow. Feel the awe and wonder and beauty of it inside your heart. Then look around you at the wet, beautiful earth and notice all the sparkling rainbows dancing on the leaves of the bushes and the petals of the flowers that are opening up. Breathe deeply and smell the wonderful scent of the wet earth, freshly nourished and cleansed by the rain.

April 5—*Grow an Experience into Being*

Perhaps you've had something on your mind for a while, something you'd like to experience in your life.

Grow this experience into being. Start with the thought in your mind and let it take root. Put your feelings into it, see it in your mind's eye before it happens, and believe with all your heart that it is already beginning to happen, gathering the energy it needs below the surface as it is in the process of coming into your life.

Grow your thought every day through your belief and happy anticipation of what is to come. Nurture the thought with positive and loving attention and actions. Be thankful that it is coming into your life and give it room to grow.

April 6—*Rebirthing Yourself*

Rebirthing yourself is sort of like a do-over, except it's much, much better because you're starting fresh from a good place, with no baggage or bad feelings.

Rebirth yourself and become the person you want to be. You're creating a brand new you—the best version of yourself.

April 7—*Dancing in the Rain*

Life isn't about waiting for the storm to pass... it's about dancing in the rain.

Embrace the storms in your life. Turn your storms into a joyful expression of the magic within you.

April 8—*Picture What You Want*

Hold the picture of what you want in your mind. Fill in the details with your feelings.

Your feelings are very powerful and will bring what you picture into being.

April 9—*Allowances*

No matter how perfectly you picture what you want, it's going to change and become even better as it gathers energy and power in the process of manifesting.

Sometimes—often—the Universe will put things into the picture that you never even thought of before—things that will enhance and make the picture of what you want even more perfect.

Hold the picture of your desired reality lightly in your mind and expect it to change—a lot.

Allow something even better than what you first envisioned to occur. Allow these changes to happen. Welcome the changes with an open mind and an open heart.

The picture just keeps getting better all the time.

April 10—*Sunny Side Up*

Look on the bright, cheerful side of things. Look for the light. Your inner self and your imagination thrive in the light.

April 11—*Replacements*

When you let go of any negative emotion or situation in your life, you need to replace the negative with something positive. You need to change your thoughts and feelings about the previous relationship or situation.

When letting go of a relationship that no longer brings you happiness, do it with love and kindness. Look at the good you've received and what you learned from the experience. This allows you to move forward in a loving manner.

When letting go of a situation that no longer serves your best interests, look at the good in what you experienced and what you learned—how it has helped you to grow.

A new relationship or situation is already forming in your life as you let go of the old, inviting and welcoming something new and positive to enter your life.

April 12—*What Were You Thinking?*

Look around at everything that is currently in your life. Look at every detail and nuance. You created all of it.

Nothing comes into your life by chance, even though at times, it may look that way. Things don't just "happen" to you.

Everything was created by a thought—by your thoughts.

April 13—*Whacking the Weeds*

Look at the experiences in your life to see how the seeds you've previously planted have come to fruition. See how they've blossomed and grown.

If you're looking at weeds, it's time to tend your garden, pull out the weeds, shake all the dirt off, and plant new seeds—seeds that will grow into harmony and joy.

April 14—*Growing a Thought*

Give your thoughts room to grow. They may be just below the surface. Let them grow, gathering energy and strength. Allow them to bud and bloom, to blossom and grow into the experiences in your life.

April 15—*Walk Away*

If someone or something makes you unhappy, walk away. Just walk away and don't give it a second thought. It's good for you. Walk toward what will make you happy.

Walk away with the knowledge that you are taking care of yourself and that you will only surround yourself with positive people and positive experiences.

If the situation or person is something big or entrenched in your life that you can't just walk away from and not look back, then begin to take the steps that will help you move away from it.

April 16—*Sleep on It*

Whenever you have something in your life you don't know how to solve, like a problem, or maybe you're unsure about something, like a choice or a decision, or you're wondering how to go about doing something, sleep on it.

Give what you're thinking about or wondering about to your subconscious mind and let your subconscious provide you with a dream that offers the perfect solution to what you were wondering about.

April 17—*Search and Rescue*

Maybe you've thought about something you wanted to do, but for whatever reason, you didn't pursue it and left the thought by the wayside. But now it's calling to you. Maybe it's just an inkling of a remembrance of a thought you let go of a long time ago. It was lost and now it's ready to be found—to be rescued.

You wonder where it went to. Look for it and find it in the recesses of your subconscious mind. It's there, hiding in the light, waiting to be seen. Bring the thought back to life. Give it energy and let it breathe.

Or maybe the thought that you thought you forgot about went and did its own thing when you weren't looking and now the thought has come to find you.

April 18—*Reclaim Your Power*

You are a powerful, positive person. No one can take your power away from you without your permission. If someone in your life makes you feel small or insignificant in some way, don't listen to them. Don't pay any attention to what they're saying. They don't know what they're talking about.

But first realize that you've allowed this to occur. Look at why you invited it into your life, then let it go. Simply disregard whatever made you feel small or insignificant, because it simply isn't true. Reclaim your power as the positive person you truly are.

April 19—*Do Something Differently*

Do the same thing differently. Just to see how it turns out.

April 20—*I Knew That Would Happen*

This most often comes into play when you're basing what you want to do on past experiences—on what has happened to you before in the past.

But it comes into play much more often when you know what will happen based on where you're going and what you're doing, and what you know will happen to bring you to your desired goal. It's also a really powerful statement that things are happening just the way you know they will.

Hey, thanks Universe! We're on the same page. We're doing a good job. I knew that would happen.

April 21—*Implement Your Ideas*

When you get an idea to do something, or you think you'd like to do something, the first thing to do is to follow your feelings and listen to your inner self.

Let your idea generate energy in the form of additional thoughts and ideas. Your inner self loves new ideas and provides you with more positive ideas to match your original idea. When your idea has generated enough energy and power, put that idea into action.

April 22—*Peaceful Power*

The nature of your subconscious mind, from which everything arises, is peaceful and quiet, gentle and nurturing. While this may seem to be subtle, the energies your subconscious mind produces are very powerful.

Your subconscious mind is the guiding force behind everything you experience. It is totally powerful, in a peaceful, loving way.

April 23—*The Best Thing—Ever!*

What's the best thing that's ever happened to you? Why was it the best thing ever? Really think about it. Bring forth your feelings about how this best thing made you feel.

Wrap these wonderful feelings all around you. Look into this best thing—ever—and see how you brought it into your life.

April 24—*Dig in the Dirt*

You may not like what I'm about to suggest, but it has to be said. There might be some negative experiences in your life you've pushed to the back of your mind and tried to forget about because the experiences were unpleasant or truly horrible. But these things have a way of coming up to the surface, no matter how hard you've tried to bury them.

You have to dig in the dirt, and get these negative experiences out and into the light of day. Look at them, understand why they happened, and why you've allowed them to occur or why you've participated in them, then joyfully toss them away.

They can no longer bother you or hurt you because you've taken away all the power they previously had over you by looking at them, understanding them, cleansing them, and then joyfully throwing them away.

They were there and now they're gone. Now you can plant clean, positive thoughts and feelings to replace the bad, dirty ones.

April 25—*It's Not a Mistake*

If something doesn't work out for you, it's because it wasn't right for you.

The Universe has an expanded, overall view and can see things you may not be aware of and will prevent you from making a mistake by showing you a new and better way to do things.

When you look at what didn't work out—and understand why it didn't work out—you're well on your way to finding a new direction, a different way of doing things, that will make whatever you want happen for your highest good.

These "seeming" mistakes could be the best thing that could have ever happened.

April 26—*Birthing a Thought*

The birth of a thought is a beautiful, wonderful, special, magical thing, appearing and coming into existence from a magical place inside you.

Treat it tenderly, with respect and awe. Welcome it into the warmth and light of your subconscious mind. Then watch this beautiful little thought grow as it births itself into what you experience in your life.

April 27—*It's for the Best*

Whatever happens, always happens for the best.

Even though you may not see it at the time, if you look back at something and reflect, you'll see that whatever happened really did happen for the best.

April 28—*Daydreaming*

Do you ever get lost in your thoughts when you're supposed to be doing something else—something you probably don't want to do—and your mind goes wandering off into more pleasant directions? Daydreaming is time well spent.

April 29—*Transformation*

Do you ever wonder about how a caterpillar transforms itself into a beautiful butterfly? About the magic that makes it happen? About what goes on inside, in the process of becoming something new and different?

Do you wonder how one thing can totally transform—change—itself into something else?

Transform your mind, your life, and your world into whoever you want to be. You have the magic within you to do this.

April 30—*Budding and Blossoming*

Notice how a flower buds, blossoms, and grows.

See yourself budding and blossoming, growing into the magical person you truly are.

Garden of Harmony

*Be in a beautiful garden filled with lush, green plants
and flowers that vibrate with health and harmony.*

Being in a beautiful garden is beneficial for your health. It promotes peace and harmony, both inside your mind and in your body, as well as uplifting your spirit.

As you read through, and then do, this meditation in your mind or outside in nature, open your imagination; enhance the meditation and add to it all the special things in nature you resonate with—the feelings that inspire and bring peace and harmony to you, and the images you feel connected to in a happy, healing way. Change the meditation in any way you want to, so it truly reflects what a garden of harmony is to you.

You may want to read this meditation when you're outside in a special place in nature where you truly feel connected with nature, so you can completely feel the healing energies of nature with every part of you—within your body, mind, and spirit—and where you can experience the vibrations of health and harmony with all your physical and spiritual senses.

You're in a very beautiful garden. Looking around, you see lush, flowering bushes filled with flowers and blooms—delicate or-

chids and multicolored wildflowers, spread among open, spacious, grassy areas. The fragrance of the flowers is lovely and pleasing; the purity of their colors is awe-inspiring.

You look at the bright, colorful, vibrant flowers swaying softly in the gentle breeze. Their colors are magnificent—shimmering and iridescent at the same time. The bushes and flowers move gently in the soft, warm breeze, creating balance and beauty within the garden and within your mind. The garden emanates a vibrant feeling of energy, radiant and abundant with life and health.

Everything in your garden vibrates in harmony, in tune with nature. It's quiet and peaceful, and the air is clean and pure and refreshing.

Deeply breathing in the peace and harmony of this beautiful, garden, you sense the oneness of the garden with nature, and you sense that same oneness within yourself as you begin to absorb the harmony and the healing energies of the garden within your body, your mind, and your spirit.

The day is filled with warm sunshine and a brilliant blue sky above you. The light and warmth of the sun on your face and body feels wonderful and rejuvenating. The green grass beneath your bare feet feels soft and luxuriant.

The healing colors of the blue sky and the green grass surround you, enveloping you with a calm, gentle, soothing, peaceful feeling. The warmth from the sun's rays begin to permeate and radiate through you, filling you with a wonderful feeling of health and harmony. You feel perfectly in tune with nature and with the universal energies of sunlight.

Within your garden, you feel drawn to a very special place of peace and harmony where you feel most in tune with the healing energies of sunlight and nature all around you. As you enter this special healing place in your garden, you feel completely at peace with yourself and totally in harmony with the beauty and serenity all around you.

In this special healing place in your garden, you feel the vibrations of energy that are both around you and within you. As you *center in on the warmth and light from the sun, you feel the healing energies of sunlight gently vibrating all around you, flowing through you and within you.*

Breathe in the sunlight; breathe in the greenness of the earth and the blueness of the sky. Breathe the health and harmony of this beautiful garden deeply inside you—into every part of your body, your mind, and your spirit.

Feel your mind, your thoughts and feelings, and your body vibrating in harmony with the light, totally in tune with both your physical and your spiritual nature, completely in tune with the peaceful, healing energies of your garden. Experience and enjoy the perfect health and harmony you feel within yourself—within your body, your mind, and your spirit.

While this meditation is very gentle, the healing energies are very powerful. Bring the peace and harmony you feel within every part of you, and the radiant vibrations of light and health you've just experienced, into your conscious mind and let them softly flow through your thoughts and feelings, and your body, over and over again.

Allow this Garden of Harmony to become a special place of healing for you whenever you need it, or when you just want to be in a pleasant place to enjoy serenity and peace of mind.

May

Imagination

May

Imagination

May 1—**Mind Pictures**

Your imagination is the most powerful resource you possess.

Through your imagination—the world of your inner images—you have the power to shape and create your outer world.

The things you envision in your mind turn out to be what you experience in your life.

Your mind-pictures are energy in motion.

Watch what you see in your imagination and you'll see that your imagination is more powerful than you ever imagined it could be.

May 2—**Put Yourself into the Picture**

Visualize what you want—whatever it may be—in great detail. Be clear, specific, and precise. Put your emotions into the picture. See, hear, touch, taste, and smell the images of what you're creating. Become totally involved. Be there. Notice how you feel when you're in the picture of your new reality.

Be in the new reality you want to experience. See yourself in your new reality, experiencing every part of it. Be completely there. See, touch, taste, hear, and smell your new reality.

The clearer and more detailed your picture is, and the more you experience it in your mind, the more the images will vibrate with energy. This will cause what you're creating to come into being sooner.

May 3—*Check it Out*

When you begin to think about what you want to do, about what you want to bring into your life, look into the possibilities of how this wonderful new thing will come into your life.

As you check out the possibilities, other related thoughts and ideas will begin to flow to you, putting themselves into the picture and grow, gathering energy, and almost before you know it, you're well on your way to creating what you want.

May 4—*A New Adventure*

Maybe there's something you should do, but for whatever reason, you don't feel like doing it right now. Maybe it's a chore or something you think is necessary at the moment, but you'd so much rather be doing something else—something that appeals to you; something that's calling to you.

Let yourself follow the flow of that thought or feeling, and do whatever is calling to you now. The other thing you're "supposed" to do will wait. Your inner self is calling to you, inviting you to explore a wonderful new adventure.

May 5—*Set Your Intent*

Visualize your end goal—what you really want to achieve or have happen in your life—in your mind—then set your intent to achieve it and make it happen. Make sure you have a clear picture of the end result you want.

An intent is like a sacred promise to yourself, and is also you letting the Universe know what you're up to so the Universe can help you achieve it. But don't sit back and wait for it to happen. Pour lots of positive energy and actions into what you want to achieve, while always holding the end goal in mind.

May 6—*Just Imagine*

Just imagine, for a moment, that your life is everything you want it to be, right here, right now. Play with that thought for a while. See what it feels like. Feel what it looks like.

Imagine that this thought—that your life is everything you want it to be—is the real thought, not an imaginary one. What does your life look like now?

May 7—*Watch Your Thoughts*

Watch your thoughts to see where they go and what they do.

Once you think them, they begin to take on a life of their own and can lead you in many wonderful directions.

May 8—*Gentle on Your Mind*

When a new idea to do something or a thought about what to do next or how to proceed, pops into your mind, let that thought or idea be gentle on your mind. Sit with it for a while.

Let it gather energy and grow, to shape and form itself into a full-fledged idea. Let it envelop you with a wonderful sense of well-being and happiness.

May 9—*Appearances Can Be Deceiving*

Acknowledge what is. See it for what it is. Accept it for what it is. Then, take another look; what looks real may not be real.

This is your starting point for making it what you want it to be, where you create what can be from what is.

May 10—*A Picture is Worth a Thousand Words*

Get a very clear picture of what you want in your mind. See it and feel it in great detail.

Title that picture with one word—to concentrate everything you want into just one word. You don't need to come up with a thousand words to describe the picture of what you want.

Put all your thoughts and emotions into the one word that perfectly describes your picture. One word is all it takes—just one magic word.

See the whole picture in your mind and associate it with that one magical, powerful word.

Then give that word to the Universe. The Universe will fill in the remaining 999 words.

May 11—*Do-Overs*

Do you ever wish you could do something over, based on *if I knew then what I know now*? Or maybe you'd like a second chance to correct past mistakes or regrets.

It's entirely possible to do this because your mind is magical.

You can reframe these events by looking at what happened differently, by changing your thoughts and feelings about it, and by viewing it differently.

When you do this, the event itself doesn't change, but your thoughts and feelings about it change, and the past event is "reframed" into a positive experience.

May 12—*Can You Imagine?*

Can you imagine what your life would be like to have what your heart desires?

If you can imagine it, then it already exists on a non-physical level and will come into your life when you begin to put your attention and awareness on whatever you can imagine.

May 13—*Can You Believe It?*

If you can believe what you see and feel in your imagination, you can create it. Belief is the key. Belief is what makes everything work.

After you imagine it, you must believe that it is real. You must believe that your desired reality is already on its way to coming into being.

May 14—*Watch Your Dreams*

Are you dreaming? Or are you awake? Morpheus (the Greek god of dreams) weaves the dreams you think you have at night when you're sleeping into what you experience in your day-to-day life.

Watch your dreams. They may become your reality.

May 15—*Out of the Clear, Blue Sky*

It's wonderful. It's magical. An idea or a thought just popped into your mind seemingly from out of nowhere, out of the clear, blue sky.

It's the answer to all the questions you've been puzzling over; it's the solution to all your problems; it's the aha moment you've been waiting for.

Where do you think the thought really came from?

May 16—*It's Just Your Imagination... Running Away With You*

Let's hope your imagination knows how to run and that it takes you with it.

May 17—*Measurements*

How do you measure success? What does success look like to you? The way you measure success is how it will come to you and how it will appear to you.

May 18—*No Problem*

The problem with problems is that you see them as problems. Ditto for worries and anything of that nature.

You are a powerful, positive person. One of the most powerful things you can do in your life is to turn any negative situation around into a positive experience. You have that power within you now. It isn't something you have to learn; it's something you already know how to do.

A problem can only exist in your life if you allow it to, if you direct negative thoughts and feelings toward the problem and energize it. When you change your perception—your thoughts and feelings—about the problem, you change the focus and direction of your energy, thereby changing how you experience the problem.

Problems are energy turned the wrong way. Turn them inside out and around, and you have a lot of energy to work with—to shape, form, and fashion in any way you choose.

May 19—*Tune In and Turn On*

First, turn off all the negative. Then, turn on all the positive and tune into the magic you have inside your mind.

May 20—*WYSIWYG*

What you see is what you get.

The pictures you see in your mind's eye are what will come into your reality in the way you see the events occurring.

If the picture you see in your mind doesn't match what you want, you might want to change the picture you see in your mind so that you'll get what you see.

May 21—*It's a Plan*

Create a plan for something you want to have happen. Give your idea or thought a good sense of direction. Imagine how it will work out.

Now you have a plan, a road map, a starting point that will take you where you want to go.

But keep in mind that plans change, and give the plan you've made room to grow.

May 22—*Follow Your Feelings*

Your feelings will always lead you in the right direction. Learn to listen to your feelings, and follow them.

May 23—*The Search for Solutions*

If there's something in your life you seem to have no control over, set your mind in motion to search for solutions.

Let your inner self show you what you can do about this "seemingly" impossible thing to change it into something that works for you.

May 24—*Magical Mirror*

Imagine you have a magical mirror in your mind that reflects your thoughts and feelings, lets you see into your situations, and shows you what you're in the process of creating.

You can use this magical mirror in every part of your life to help you see, create, or change anything you want. Just use your imagination.

May 25—*Feed Your Imagination*

It's starving for positive thoughts and feelings. Feed it the good stuff.

May 26—*Wandering Thoughts*

Let your thoughts wander. See where they take you.

May 27—*Read Between the Lines*

Read between the lines of what you are experiencing to see what's really happening in your experiences below the surface.

There is so much happening that you can't see which isn't apparent on the surface.

May 28—*Adopt an Attitude*

Imagine that you're happy, healthy, successful, whatever, and adopt that attitude for today, maybe forever.

Pretty soon, you'll discover that you really are happy, healthy, successful, or whatever.

Your subconscious mind doesn't know you're pretending. It believes everything you think and say, and will act on your adopted attitude as if it is the real thing.

And then another amazing thing happens. The attitude you adopted is no longer adopted. It's yours and it belongs to you.

May 29—*Starting From Scratch*

Perhaps you're ready to do something entirely new—something you've never done before, and you're not entirely sure how to proceed. And maybe you're feeling a little overwhelmed about starting from scratch.

Everything has to begin somewhere, from a tiny thought, feeling, or idea which grows into something magical and magnificent.

It all begins with a thought inside your mind. Let that thought grow and show you how to start from scratch.

May 30—*The Shape of Things to Come*

You probably have a pretty clear picture of how things are shaping up because of what you're currently experiencing.

Allow a picture to form in your mind of the shape of things to come. See what will probably happen and what other things come into your picture that are in the process of shaping and forming themselves into your experiences.

May 31—*Got Questions? Get Answers*

You wouldn't be able to ask the question if you didn't already know the answer.

Got questions? Your inner self has the answers.

June

Seeding Your Subconscious

June

Seeding Your Subconscious

June 1—*Today is a Great Day!*

What you think and believe turns out to be what you experience. What you expect to happen, will happen.

Tell yourself that today is going to be a great day. No matter what happened yesterday, or what you have planned for today, or what you think may happen today, simply tell yourself, "Today is going to be a great day!"

Put your whole heart and soul into it. Say it with lots of positive feelings and an absolute belief in the truth of your statement. This simple sentence will create a great day for you. It works through your positive attitude because you are creating a great day for yourself.

You'll be opening yourself up to wonderful experiences and allowing really great things to happen. You'll be allowing the magic of your mind to create a wonderful day for you. And you may even experience a few happy surprises. Try it and see what happens!

June 2—*A Brand New Idea*

A totally new idea, one you've never thought of before, has just popped into your mind and presented itself to you.

You really like the idea. It totally appeals to you. Explore that idea and see where it takes you.

June 3—*Awesome Affirmations*

"I am perfectly healthy."

"I am totally awesome."

"I am… you fill in the blank."

Create your own list of awesome affirmations that fit your lifestyle and are apropos to what you want to experience in your life and what you want to achieve.

Choose affirmations that ring true for you and validate who you are.

June 4—*Can You Do It?*

If at first, you think you can't do something—maybe you feel it's too big or too much to handle—think again.

Whatever it is, you can do it. The thought wouldn't enter your mind if you couldn't.

It's entirely possible. You can do it.

June 5—*Attention*

Devote your full, undivided attention to whatever you are doing in the moment. Be fully present.

Don't scatter your energies. All the other thoughts about things you want to do will wait. That's one of the nice things about thoughts. They will patiently wait their turn for your full, undivided attention.

June 6—*What Were You Expecting?*

Sometimes we get what we think we don't want. Look into what you were expecting and you'll see that you got what you expected, even if you didn't think that was what you wanted. This can be a good thing or a bad thing.

Your expectations set the stage for what comes into your life. Look into your expectations to see what's coming your way. If you don't like what you see, change your expectations so you can expect to get what you truly want.

June 7—*You Are More Than Good Enough*

You are more than good enough. In fact, you're so much better than good enough.

June 8—*Drawing Magical Mind Pictures*

Visualize what you want to achieve. See it in your mind's eye in great detail. Feel the emotions inside the picture. Make the picture perfect; make it everything you want it to be. See yourself achieving it.

As you do this, you will draw into your life all the energy that it needs to make it happen. See it, believe it, achieve it.

June 9—*It's Definitely Doable*

You can do this! Whatever it is, you can do it! It's definitely doable! Tell yourself every day that you can do it!

Believe in yourself and in your ability to create what you want.

Grow that belief into action and do what is definitely doable.

June 10—*What do You Think?*

Everyone has an opinion on everything, from the way to do things, to perhaps the way you "should" do things, to the way that's best for you.

Maybe people can offer good advice, but that advice is always based on their experiences and feelings.

What's your opinion? What do you think? What is best for you?

June 11—*Attitude is Everything*

The way you go about doing things is the same way you will achieve them. Attitude is everything. A positive attitude is the key to opening all the wonderful, magical treasures you have inside you A positive attitude will open doorways and shine a light on your path.

On the other side of that is a negative attitude. You can still achieve things with a negative attitude, if that's your choice, but it will be a long, slow process, fraught with anxiety and despair, and you may not like what you get.

Choose the positive attitude. The reality you want depends on it.

June 12—*I'm Getting There!*

Yes, you are. You're getting there. Sometimes the journey to get what you truly want takes a little bit longer than you originally thought. That's because so many wonderful things happen along the way.

Keep going. Keep the end in sight. You'll get there.

June 13—*Good Intentions*

The road to you-know-where is paved with good intentions.

All those good intentions were never filled with positive energy and actions; that's why they never went where they were supposed to go.

Put positive energy inside your good intentions and **act** on them. They'll pave the way to a really good place.

June 14—*Better, Better, and Better*

"Every day, and in every way, I am better, better, and better."

These are very powerful words and span a multitude of uses—for healing, for situations, and for relationships.

Better, better, and better.

June 15—*It's Working!*

See what's working—and what isn't working.

Direct your energies—your thoughts and feelings—toward what *is* working.

June 16—*Multi-Tasking*

Doing two things at once can be a little challenging. If you're trying to manifest too many things at the same time, you could get your wires crossed or at the very least, scatter the energies and slow down the process of getting what you want.

Might be a good idea to devote your full attention to one thing at a time.

However, the Universe is very good at multi-tasking, and may just surprise you with granting you everything you want at the same time.

June 17—*Watch What You Say*

Words have power. They have the power to make or break whatever you're thinking about or experiencing. Watch what you say.

Be even more vigilant about what you don't say. Pay attention to the feeling of the words and what the feelings say.

June 18—*Listen to the Words*

Listen to the words you say and what feelings they inspire inside you. If the words you say are making you happy, keep on saying them.

If your words bring forth negative feelings inside you, it's time to change the words.

June 19—*Plant Positive Thoughts*

Thoughts can change any experience. A thought can completely turn around any situation. A thought is a very powerful thing. Plant positive thoughts and watch them grow. Your wonderful new reality depends on it.

June 20—*Don't Go There*

Don't go to places like wallowing, self-pity, a feeling of helplessness, and sadness—places that are filled with despair.

Why would you even want to go there when there are so many much nicer places to visit, like laughter, love, joy, and happiness?

Don't go to dark, isolated, scary places. The accommodations are terrible, dark, and cold.

Go to places that are warm and welcoming, places that are filled with light and happiness. The accommodations are wonderful.

When you feel despairing, go to a place called hope. When you feel yourself getting angry, go to a place called peace. When you feel helpless, go to a place called power.

When you feel any negativity pulling you into a bad place, go to the good places instead.

June 21—**Bits and Pieces**

It's perfectly okay to not know exactly where you're going or how you're going to get there. You just know you'll find a way or that a way will show itself to you.

Many times, information or answers you want come to you in bits and pieces, in flashes of intuition or sparkles of insight, or in dreams, and the whole picture isn't quite clear at the moment.

This information has a really nice habit of happening on a regular basis, and pretty soon you've got all the pieces of the picture, and can put it together perfectly.

June 22—**Second Thoughts**

If the same thought keeps repeating itself in your mind, you might want to pay attention to it.

The thought presents itself numerous times until it has your attention and you begin to act on it.

Think of it as gentle nudges from your inner self.

June 23—**Are You Out of Your Mind?**

Watch what comes out of your mind. The thoughts that rise unbidden. The feelings that show themselves.

Watch the thoughts that come out of your mind.

June 24—*Rephrasing*

Watch the way you talk, the words that appear in your mind, and the way you phrase words in sentences. Sometimes, without meaning to, you may say something you think is positive, but it's actually negative.

The giveaway is that you're placing emphasis on the negative by using words like can't, won't, couldn't, shouldn't, and wouldn't. The negative contractions will stop whatever you're creating dead in its tracks.

Watch the way you phrase your sentences and the words you use. Use the opposite of the negative to create the positive.

June 25—*Everything is Working Out Perfectly*

If you're involved in a situation that seems impossible, and you don't know what to do about it or how to get yourself out of it, or when something in your life appears to be going the wrong way or moving in a direction you think you don't want, tell yourself that "everything is working out perfectly."

There's always a higher reason that you may not be aware of at the moment, but when you believe that everything is working out perfectly, then everything does work out perfectly, even if you haven't got a clue how to proceed or how the situation will work itself out.

June 26—*Too Much on Your Mind*

You have sooo many things on your mind that you want to do and accomplish. Really good, wonderful things. You can see them all in your mind, you know you're going to do them; that they're going to happen, but you just don't know when you'll find the time to do them all.

Your thoughts are all coming together at once, crowding your mind and begging for attention. You have to make a choice. You can't answer to them all at the same time. Some of them will have to wait.

Talk to your thoughts and tell them you'll be happy to do whatever they want (it's actually what you want), but it's a matter of timing. Let them know they still need to grow and that they'll come into fruition when the time is right. Let them know you'll take them, one by one, and make them happen.

Some of your thoughts are probably calling to you more strongly than others. These are the ones that have probably been on your mind for a long time, or have something very important to tell you.

Choose the thoughts you feel most in tune with at the moment. Go with them and grow with them.

Then go with the next thought, and the next one. You have a never-ending supply of thoughts. Choose the ones that can grow with you and can grow you.

June 27—**Seven Seeds**

Ideas to plant in your subconscious mind:

1. Imagination will grow beautiful mind pictures.

2. Gratitude will grow joy and bloom into magic.

3. Appreciation will grow into harmony and what you love.

4. Expectation will grow into all sorts of wonderful things happening in your life.

5. Accepting will grow into getting in the flow, recognizing all the good in your life, and drawing even more good into your life.

6. Positivity will absolutely proliferate and grow into a magical life, filled with happiness and light.

7. Intuition will grow into learning how to trust yourself and how to listen to your inner self, and how to follow your feelings.

June 28—**Stay Focused**

It's so tempting and easy to get sidetracked, to get pulled away from what you're creating and to lose sight of your goal. A new idea comes along and calls to you or you get an urge to do something else.

Stay on course. The little sidetracks you're experiencing along the way are new thoughts that are in the process of forming; ones that will be happening in the future. They just wanted to say "hi." They'll wait patiently and be there when you're ready to give them the full attention they deserve.

June 29—*What Would You Like to Do Today?*

Today is your special day of power. You can do anything you want to do. Today is a day of power, where everything you imagine becomes real, and everything you think about happens.

Everything you do today—and every day—is powerful.

June 30—*The Right Way*

There is a right way to do things and a wrong way.

If someone tries to tell you that their way is the right way, that's their perception—not yours. That's their choice of how to do things. That's their way, not your way.

Just smile at them because you know better. You know how to do things the right way.

July

Freedom ~ Letting Go

July

Freedom ~ Letting Go

July 1—**Being Free**

Allow yourself to be free, to let go of anything that might be holding you back. Let yourself go with the flow, and explore wonderful new possibilities.

July 2—**Holding Back**

If you're not achieving something you want, look at what is possibly holding you back from what you want to accomplish. It may be something invisible, and you may only be aware of it as an uneasy feeling, something that doesn't feel quite right.

What is holding you back from being truly happy and successful? When you discover what it is, let it go and move forward.

July 3—**Something New**

Try something new—something you've never done before. Just for the heck of it. Just to see what happens.

July 4—**Freedom**

What if, today, all your cares and worries were gone? Disappeared into thin air? Totally, completely, not there anymore?

What if, today, all your responsibilities and problems simply didn't exist? What if, today, you could just be you, free and light? What if, today, you could just be joy?

July 5—*Are We There Yet?*

Sometimes you might get so focused on getting what you want that you don't always enjoy the journey of getting there. And sometimes you might get a little impatient if your goal doesn't manifest soon enough.

Might be fun to just simply enjoy all the little things along the way as you're arriving where you want to go.

July 6—*Treasures*

If your house was burning and you could save only ONE thing, what would it be? Why would you save it? Why do you treasure it?

If all your emotions were taken away from you except for ONE emotion you could still have, what would that emotion be? Why would you keep that emotion inside you? Why is that emotion something you treasure?

July 7—*It's Really Happening!*

WooHoo! It's happening. It's really happening! The new reality you've created for yourself in your mind is beginning to appear in your life. Of course it is! You created it and set it into motion and made it happen through your thoughts, feelings, and actions.

It's so exciting to see a goal begin to manifest—to come into being. Be absolutely delighted and revel in your new reality. Really feel the excitement and happiness. It's really happening!

July 8—*Horizons*

Something new looms on the horizon—a wonderful new adventure. It's just around the corner, waiting to appear in your life. You may not even be fully aware of it yet, or it may come as a complete surprise.

July 9—*I Don't Know Yet*

It is perfectly okay to not have all the answers, or to be unsure of which way you want to go. It's even okay to feel a little lost now and then.

Your inner self has all the answers. Your inner self is sure about which way to go. Your inner self never gets lost.

Maybe now is a good time to talk to your inner self. Your inner self really likes you and wants to help you in every way.

July 10—*Forgiveness*

Some things need to be forgiven. Some hurts need to be healed. Look at whatever it is to see the good in it—what you learned from the experience and how it has helped you to grow.

Thank it for being in your life, accept the lesson, bless it, and let the bad go.

You feel so free and light once you've forgiven whatever needs to be forgiven. It can only hurt you if you hang on to it. Let it go.

July 11—*I Doubt It*

Don't put doubt into the picture of what you're creating. Worrying about whether something will happen or doubting if it ever will happen, will stop whatever you're in the process of creating. It will come to a screeching halt.

If you doubt it, it won't happen. That's a definite.

Push doubt and worry away. They're merely shadows with no substance. They have no place in your magical mind and in your power as a creator.

July 12—*Go With the Flow*

Let your mind take you where it will. It knows where it's going and how to get there, and it's taking you along for the ride.

Just go with the flow and enjoy the scenery along the way.

July 13—*What do You Want?*

What do you really want? Think about it for a while.

When you know what you really want, and you feel it inside you, the energy of that thought begins to change into showing you avenues to explore so you can have what you really want.

July 14—*No Excuses*

There's no need to make excuses for something you don't want to do or for whatever is happening in your life. These "excuses" are really "explanations" which show you the power you have to look at all your experiences honestly and with an open mind.

You'll see that explanations provide you with so much more material to work with than excuses, and offer insights and understanding into yourself on a positive level.

July 15—*It's Not True*

Perhaps you're just beginning to work on a new goal—creating a new reality for yourself—something that is in the early stages of growing or you're doing something you've never done before. Take care of this precious thought.

If someone tells you that you can't do something, or that something is too hard, or that you'll never achieve it, don't listen to them. It's not true. You can do whatever you want. You can make difficult things a wonderful challenge, and you can achieve what you want.

July 16—*A Note to Yourself*

Dear me, a year from now…

If you could leave a note for your "self" to read in the future, what would you say to yourself?

July 17—*A Note from Yourself*

Hello, grown-up me…

If you could read a note from your younger self, what would the note say? What does your younger self have to tell you?

July 18—*A Note from Your Future Self*

Hey there, it's me...

Imagine you're reading a note from your future self. What does the note say? What does your future self want you to know?

July 19—*Observe*

Close your eyes and watch your thoughts, listen to what they say, see what they show you. Then open your eyes and watch the images of your thoughts that are all around you, everywhere.

July 20—*A Watchful Eye*

Just for today, or maybe for a few hours, watch yourself as you go through your day. Watch how you feel and respond to the situations you encounter and the experiences you have as they unfold.

Look into your feelings as you're watching your experiences. Watch yourself as you watch your life play out.

Just simply observe for a while. Watch yourself as if you are observing someone else—seeing yourself through their eyes. Watch yourself to see how your inner self sees you.

July 21—*The Point of No Return*

Once you become a truly positive person—one who sees the joy and light in everything, and has a wonderful attitude toward everything that happens—there's no turning back.

You are a truly positive person. It only gets better from this point forward.

July 22—*Exploring New Ideas*

Be open to exploring new ideas that float into your mind seemingly from out of nowhere. Be open and flexible to the ideas and insights from your inner self.

Listen to your inner self whispering to you in all your thoughts, reminding you of the magic within yourself.

July 23—*No Worries*

Worry has no place in your beautiful mind. Let your worries go so that there are no worries in your mind—and in your life.

July 24—*Be Prepared*

Not everyone is going to like what you're doing or the new reality you're experiencing. Be prepared for this. Maybe they're a bit jealous or envious of your success.

Truth of the matter is: As long as *you* like your new reality and the way you go about doing things, you're fine.

Just be prepared for the people who aren't fine with it. Tell them it works for you; it doesn't have to work for them. Tell them you're happy with the way things are going and how you're achieving what you want.

Try to understand where they're coming from and why they feel the way they do, then see if you can lend a helping hand. If they don't want or need your help, then bless them and let them go their own way.

July 25—*You Can Do Anything You Want to Do*

It's your life. You choose how to live it, what you do, what you want to experience, and how you want to experience it.

You are totally free to do whatever you want—to do anything your heart desires.

Let go of any shadows that may be blocking your light, or any limits or judgments that you or others have placed on you that may be holding you back from being completely free and living your life in a wonderful and joyful manner.

July 26—*Being Quiet*

Sometimes it's important to step back from everything and just be quiet. Take some time to breathe and be. Take some peaceful time for yourself. In this quiet place, you can hear yourself think and can become clear on what's on your mind.

July 27—*Listening*

Listen to the voice within that is always trying to tell you something special. Your inner self knows what's best for you and what thoughts will bring you happiness and joy.

All you have to do is listen to what your inner self says.

July 28—*Self-Sabotage*

If things aren't working out for you in the way you want them to, look into your subconscious mind to find out why.

There could be fears lurking there, buried deep below the surface, or an unconscious belief you hold that you're not even aware of which prevents you from achieving what you want.

Sometimes the greatest self-sabotage tool in your unconscious mind is fear—fear of success. If you succeed in what you want, you will have to make big changes—changes that will alter the course of your life.

You'll have to let go of the familiar and the comfortable, and enter unfamiliar and uncharted territory. It's second nature, sometimes, to resist change. A fear of the unknown, or not knowing what will happen, may sabotage your steps toward what you want.

Really look—honestly and openly—at what is preventing you from getting what you want. When you see what it is, you know you have the power to change that—to turn the energy around to help you, rather than hinder you.

July 29—*Highs and Lows*

You're going to have days where everything works out perfectly and days where it seems nothing much is happening, or everything seems to be going wrong. It only seems that way.

This is normal and to be expected. Something is always happening, whether you're aware of it or not.

And sometimes you just need to take a break so that whatever you're working on has room to breathe and grow, to become the good thing it is meant to be.

July 30—*Just for Fun*

Do something today that is just for fun. Just because it appeals to you and you want to do it. Do it for no other reason than it's fun.

July 31—*It'll Pass*

Whatever you're experiencing—especially if it's something negative you seem to have no control over—will pass.

It's only temporary, a glitch, a bump in the road.

Keep your spirits up and look ahead. Whatever is bothering you at the moment will pass.

And when it passes, it will leave behind something you couldn't see before—a gift maybe you didn't recognize or a direction that wasn't visible before.

August

Perspectives and Perceptions

August

Perspectives and Perceptions

August 1—*It's Easy*

Some things in life do require hard work and may take a long time to manifest exactly the way you want them to.

Make it easy on yourself. View the hard work as what it really is—a joy. Experience the time it takes as a wonderful journey.

It's easy.

August 2—*Intangibles*

Sometimes people think of creating their reality as getting material things—tangible things you can see and touch on a physical level—like a new car, a house, a new relationship, a better job, things of that nature.

While all these things are nice and very wonderful, and are part of creating your reality, the true part of creating your reality is often the intangible things you want and already have, such as a sense of pride in what you do, being happy with your life, loving the people you are with, and things of that nature.

Often the intangible things are the most valuable. Look at the intangibles in your life—the things you can't physically see or touch—to see how real they are and how they permeate all aspects of your life.

And one more thing about intangibles: They have a very nice habit of turning into tangibles.

August 3—*Magical Messages*

With your eyes closed, open this book or any book, or a newspaper, or a magazine. Let your finger rest on the page, then open your eyes to the words your inner self has chosen for you to read, seemingly by chance or at random. This is your magical message for the day.

Let the words your magical mind has chosen for you, and their meaning, be gentle on your mind for a few moments. Ponder their magical significance. Let them show you what you need to see; let them tell you what you need to hear.

Listen with your heart, mind, and soul to the meaning of the words. Listen to what your inner self is saying to you.

Perhaps the words will inspire pictures or an image in your mind. Perhaps the words will create or bring forth a feeling within you that will open an inner awareness.

Perhaps the words will offer you a direction or give you a purpose for the day. Perhaps they will instruct you to do something or give you a clear answer to a question you have.

August 4—*Ups and Downs*

One day you're zinging along, happy as can be, and everything is working perfectly, everything is falling into place. The next day, you feel as if nothing is working properly.

It happens. The "up" can't exist without the "down." It's a balancing act.

Put more of your energy into the "up." The "down" will dissipate and may also give you a respite and some much-needed time to regroup and focus on the "up."

August 5—*The Night Isn't Black if You Know That It's Green*

What do you suppose this means? That reality is only an illusion? That what we choose to believe makes something real? That truth is how we see it? That our feelings define our perception?

What do you think?

August 6—*Past Tense*

Put negative thoughts and feelings in the past. Phrase those thoughts and feelings in the past tense, i.e., "I did feel that way; not anymore. I did think that; now I've changed my mind."

This puts negativity in its proper place—behind you. It's in the past.

August 7—*Play With Your Thoughts*

Play with your thoughts when they come to you, bubbling up from your subconscious mind, to see what they show you.

Your subconscious likes to play; it's one of the things it does best. So, play with your thoughts to see where they take you. This is a lot of fun and can show you things you may not have been aware of before.

Playing with your thoughts opens new avenues for you to explore.

August 8—*Subtle Signs*

Subtle signs… or maybe not so subtle if you know what to look for. Very often—more often than not—your inner self shows you signs and offers you a direction to go in that perhaps you weren't seeing clearly before.

Look for the deeper meaning of an experience. See what isn't working. You'll soon realize what is really happening, and what your inner self is trying to tell you.

See things in a new light; put new ideas and fresh perspectives into the experience to take it in an entirely different direction.

These signs from your inner self are often shown to you in a symbolic manner. All you need to do is clearly look at and into your experiences to see what they're really showing you and saying to you.

What has your inner self shown you recently?

August 9—*Viewpoints*

Everyone has an opinion and may try to impose their opinion or their way of thinking on you. What works for them may or may not work for you.

Listen to your own opinion and follow your own advice. You've got the best viewpoint. It was born in your magical mind.

August 10—*Seeing Clearly*

Look through things as they **seem** to be to see them as they really are.

August 11—*Dealing With Disappointment*

It happens. It's happened before and it will happen again.

The way in which you deal with disappointment determines whether you will continue to feel disappointed when something doesn't work out the way you want it to or hope it will, or whether you will view disappointment as a necessary stepping stone that leads you into getting what you want.

Disappointment may actually provide you with a much better, more vibrant way of doing things.

August 12—*Look Inside Your Dreams*

Your dreams are a wonderful and powerful resource you have available to you every night. They invite you into a nighttime panorama of pictures played on the screen of your subconscious mind.

Your inner self lives inside your mind and softly walks through your dream world.

Dreams provide you with a rich resource of information, answers, and insights. They can guide you in your life. Look inside your dreams. Listen to your dreaming self.

August 13—*Perceptions*

Open the magic inside your mind by changing and re-arranging the way you look at and perceive things. By doing this, you'll get a wonderful glimpse into the magical power of your mind and your imagination.

You have the power to turn the mundane into the magical, the ordinary into the extraordinary, and the blahs into the blissful, simply by the way you perceive things.

August 14—*Approach*

Look at how you approach doing new things. When you think of something you'd like to do, does it fill you with energy and excitement? Can you hardly wait to get started?

Can you feel your mind humming with the possibilities and opening avenues for you to explore? Do you jump right in and start doing it, full speed ahead?

Or does doing something new fill you with a feeling of trepidation, wondering how you'll ever accomplish it? Take a breath and take a new approach.

Before you know it, you'll be zipping along, filled with energy and excitement about accomplishing this new thing.

August 15—*Detours Along the Way*

Sometimes a detour—instead of deterring you—can lead you onto a new path—a different direction—and show you entirely new perspectives and adventures, and possibly a way to change your thinking.

Maybe a detour is exactly what you need to show you where you need to go.

August 16—*Sidetracks*

If you think you're getting sidetracked away from what you want to achieve, perhaps what you perceive as a sidetrack is really a side trip into a new or different way to do things.

It's always interesting, and often very enlightening, to see where your mind, and the Universe, takes you, and the direction it takes to provide you with exactly what you want and need.

August 17—*Silent Signals*

Sometimes, without meaning to, you can send yourself silent, almost imperceptible signals that sabotage all your positive efforts.

Learn to listen to and see what these silent signals are saying to you so you can stop them in their tracks before they destroy all your good work.

Look inside your unconscious feelings to ferret them out.

August 18—*In Awe*

Look at something you see every day, something that's perhaps a bit ordinary or commonplace. Now, look at it in awe and wonder to see the true magic and magnificence of it. Sense the energy within it.

This is the way your inner self sees it—as it truly is—wonderful and beautiful and special.

August 19—*What's So Funny?*

Every situation—especially the negative ones—have an absurd, hilarious side. Look for the humor in the bad stuff of what you are experiencing to see what's funny about it. It's always there.

If you can laugh at what is happening, and see the humor in it, you can gain good insights into what is really happening in the experience, and you can see what you need to do to change it on a lighthearted level.

Laughter will bring your energies back up to a positive level.

August 20—*It's All the Same*

The way you see and feel about things—how you perceive them—in your life is the same exact way you will experience them.

Negative attracts negative. Positive attracts positive.

If you doubt that certain things will ever happen, they won't. If you think things will work out, they will.

August 21—*Perfect Timing*

Synchronicity is the simultaneous occurrence of events which appear significantly related but have no discernible cause. It's like perfect timing when everything comes together.

Or maybe you prefer to call it serendipity, which is the occurrence and development of events by chance in a happy or beneficial way.

Whatever you call it, it happens because you create certain events to occur as you direct your energy toward achieving a goal, and the Universe responds by creating these events to occur at the perfect time.

It's also a sign and a confirmation that you're on the right path.

August 22—*Chatter*

Listen to the chatter in your mind for one full minute. Just stop whatever you are doing and listen, really listen.

You'll be amazed at how many thoughts run rampant through your mind.

And listen to your self-talk; the things you tell yourself when you think you're not listening. Words that are spoken through your feelings.

August 23—*That Didn't Work Out the Way I Thought it Would.*

When you think you're doing everything right and your desired reality fails to manifest, look into the why of it.

There's always a reason you didn't get what you thought you wanted. Perhaps there were some negative doubts mixed in with what you thought you wanted.

Perhaps it means that what you wanted wasn't for your highest good and the Universe stepped in to stop you before you made a mistake.

When something doesn't work out the way you wanted it to or hoped it would, understand the message the Universe is giving you and plot a new course to achieve what you want.

August 24—*How Do You See Yourself?*

The way you see yourself is reflected in the way you act and the things you do, and how you project yourself to others.

How do you see yourself?

August 25—*It's All Good*

Whatever is happening is always for your highest good.

When you experience negative situations in your life, remember that it's all good.

Look for and find the good in every situation.

August 26—*I Take Great Pride in That*

Really feel the pride you feel when you achieve something—whether it's big or small. Be very proud of yourself and what you've accomplished.

Be proud of everything you've achieved so far.

Take pride in everything you do.

August 27—*Expect the Unexpected*

It happens. Every. Single. Time. The unexpected will occur, showing up as a surprise (unless you were expecting it). Count on it. Without fail, you'll find a few or more unexpected things come into your reality. This happens for a few reasons:

One is that the Universe sees the entire picture of what you're creating that sometimes you can't clearly see, and will toss things your way to help you out.

The second reason might be because you have an open mind—which is a good thing—and you've allowed for wonderful things to happen that you may not have consciously put into the picture, but are willing to accept as they unfold.

Another reason is because unexpected things occur to show you that you need to revise your original goal or to give you a chance to second-think your original approach.

The unexpected is always a good thing. Look for the unexpected and welcome it with open arms. The unexpected will always come as a gift—to show you new and better ways of doing things, to gently encourage you to make changes.

August 28—*It's Entirely Possible*

Just because it's never happened before, and you might think it can't happen, doesn't mean that it won't happen.

Whatever you want is entirely possible. Change your thoughts, beliefs, and your attitude. Make it possible. Make it happen.

Generate lots of positive energy and action toward what you want to happen.

August 29—*Hope*

Do you often find yourself hoping that something will happen?

Toss hope out the window. Hope isn't going to get you anywhere. Hope is only telling you that it's possible. You're the one who actually has to do the work.

Hoping is a nice thought, but hoping won't make it happen.

August 30—*A Miracle in the Making*

Your life is a miracle in the making. Miracles are all around you, everywhere, every day, and in every experience—even in the most ordinary places and mundane moments.

Look around you at all the wonderful miracles you see in every moment of your life—in every thought, feeling, and experience you have.

August 31—**Look Within**

Look inside your mind. Look into your imagination to see your intuition and insights—to see and read the signs from your inner self—and to recognize the inner knowing you have within you.

Play with your thoughts, change the way you look at things, and watch them grow into your experiences.

September

Creating Your Reality

September

Creating Your Reality

September 1—**Creation**

You are a very powerful creator. You orchestrate all your experiences and you control the energies to make your experiences whatever you want them to be.

You create everything you experience in your life through your thoughts and feelings. You draw people and situations and experiences to you.

You will bring into your life whatever you envision in the way you perceive it and believe it. Through your imagination, and your thoughts and feelings, followed by your actions, you shape your reality into existence.

September 2—**Finding Your Focus**

Set a new goal—something you want to achieve. Align your energies—your thoughts and feelings—toward what you want.

Focus your intention and energy to create what you want to experience in your reality.

Keep your focus clear and aimed toward your goal. Fluff off anything that deters and distracts you. Keep focused on what you want.

September 3—*Mirror Reflections*

Your reality is a mirror of your thoughts and feelings. The situations, experiences, and people in your life are mirror reflections of your thoughts and feelings.

Everything you are experiencing in your life now is a reflection of your previous thoughts, feelings, and actions.

Look at what is all around you to see what you've created—to see how the thoughts you think and the feelings you feel have turned into your present reality that is reflecting your thoughts and feelings back to you.

September 4—*Reality is an Illusion*

Before something becomes real—before it becomes visible in your life—it appears in your mind as a thought or in your heart as a feeling. It's invisible; it's an illusion because it isn't yet real on a physical level where you can see it and touch it.

The end result—something you can see and feel—is first created in your mind and in your heart where it appears to be an illusion.

The invisible becomes visible. The illusion becomes the reality. That's why reality is so illusionary.

September 5—*Respect*

You have a tremendous amount of power. Use it wisely and respect the power you have.

Make sure that whatever you want or are in the process of manifesting is for the highest good of all who will be touched by it or involved it in.

September 6—*Hang in There*

It's going to happen—whatever you want. Sometimes—for whatever reason—you can't see the whole picture at the moment. Just hang in there and keep feeding your positive thoughts with energy and attention.

Don't demand that your new reality happen right this minute. Your subconscious mind and the Universe don't like demands. Other things may have to happen first to bring your desired reality into being.

Step-by-step, one foot in front of the other, will make it happen. Don't let doubt or discouragement stand in your way.

Keep the faith. Hang in there. It'll happen.

September 7—*Dream a New Dream*

You can make your dreams come true.

It's been said that we dream our life into being, and that life is as you dream it.

If your life isn't exactly the way you want it to be, dream a different dream. Dream your life differently; do your life differently.

Dream an experience you really want into being—whatever that experience may be—perhaps a more loving relationship, a new job, painting a picture, writing a book, moving to Hawaii, adopting a dog, buying a house, composing a symphony, or simply being happy, whatever your dream is.

Dream a magical dream. Dream that your life is everything you want it to be, right here, right now, and live that dream.

Everything is perfect; everything is awesome. You are living a dream come true.

Weave that dream into the fabric of your life.

September 8—*Walk the Talk*

Everything you think, do, and say matters. It must match and be in harmony. This will create positive and powerful energies to flow to you.

If what you think, say, and do is contradictory and isn't in harmony, then the energies are scattered and go every which way, not necessarily the way you want them to go.

Walk your talk. You're showing your subconscious, and the Universe, that you're serious about what you want to happen, and you're sincere in wanting it. This connects the energies and gives you a clear pathway to getting what you truly want.

September 9—*A Self-Fulfilling Prophecy*

Whatever you think about, you cause to occur. Whether the thought is negative or positive, you will experience the energy repercussions of that thought in your experiences.

Always, always think positive thoughts to fulfill a prophecy of happiness and light in whatever you experience.

September 10—*Adoption*

Adopt something new. Adopt a new habit, attitude, belief, or whatever, for today. Wear it within your mind and in your outer experiences.

Act as if your new "adoption" is really the way things are. Try it on for size and see if it fits into your life.

September 11—*Mind Movies*

You are the writer, actor, director, producer, and star of your life. You write the script of all your experiences, you act the part, you direct your actions, and you produce the movie that is your life in motion.

You have the magical ability and power to write, act, direct, produce, and star in the story of your life.

September 12—*Manifesting What's on Your Mind*

The secret to manifesting what you want is to make it real first in your mind, then put positive energy into it and watch it appear in your life.

Think about what you want, play with your thoughts and feelings about it, put your absolute belief into it, then imagine it as already real.

The magic that makes it work is because you see something that does not yet exist as something that does already exist.

September 13—*Wannabes*

I wannabe rich, successful, happy, etc., whatever you wannabe.

This is the first step toward creating what you want.

Make your wannabe happen.

September 14—*Reasons*

Everything happens for a reason. It's always for the highest good, even though it may not seem like it at the time. Look inside an experience to see the "real" reason it happened.

You may surprise yourself with what you see. Perhaps at the time this experience happened, you couldn't understand the reasons for it, but now it makes perfect sense, and it's helped to bring you to where you are now.

September 15—*Directions*

Move toward what you want, rather than moving away from what you don't want. The distinction is very subtle, but it makes a world of difference in how you direct your energies.

If you're moving away from what you don't want, you're reinforcing the negative and directing your energy toward what you don't want.

Your results will follow the flow of your energy and you'll find that the negative is what you end up with. By moving away from what you don't want, you get what you wanted to get rid of.

When you move toward what you want, you energize the positive. You direct your energy in a positive way and experience positive results. You get what you really want.

September 16—*Rethinking*

If something isn't working out to your liking, you might want to rethink it—to see how it *could* work out by looking into other possibilities or taking it in a different direction. Rethink, reframe, and rephrase your thoughts.

September 17—*Timing*

Set a time frame in which to accomplish something. This gives you a road map for creating what you want to accomplish as you gather the energies necessary to achieve what you want.

But be careful with this. If you give yourself too much time to reach your goal, you may tend to think you've got plenty of time and might busy yourself with other things, thinking you'll get back to it later.

If you're wishy-washy about it, the Universe will take notice and be flaky about it, too. The Universe is just following your lead.

If you give yourself too little time, you might think you can push yourself to reaching your goal, but all you'll accomplish is stressing yourself out and rushing yourself, and creating a not-so-nice mindset.

Timing is important. Give it some careful thought. You do need to create a time frame in which something will manifest, or it will just float around forever. Set your intention with a reasonable time frame.

September 18—*The Power of Secrecy*

Can you keep a secret? Secrecy builds energy and power that you can direct toward what you want. If you "spill the beans" so to speak, you'll be diluting the energy.

You might fall prey to someone else's negative opinion if you share what's on your mind that you're thinking about creating.

Be quiet about what you really want until it's strong enough to stand on its own.

September 19—*Substitutions*

Reality is an ever-flowing, always-changing energy, totally open to change and willing to accept substitutions.

If something isn't working in your life, substitute it for something that will work.

It's easy. Just change your mind.

September 20—*Let 'er Rip*

Put all your energy, and your whole heart and soul, into something that is important to you. When you do that, the Universe will match your energies and intention.

September 21—*Every. Single. Day.*

Creating your reality isn't some mystical, elusive concept. It's something you do every day.

You already know how to create your reality because you do it every single day—with your thoughts, your attitude, how you act and react to the experiences in your life, and through your feelings about everything.

You even create your reality in your dreams when you think you are sleeping.

September 22—*Seeing Things That Aren't There*

When you can see things that aren't there, you're more than hallway home to creating what you want and bringing it into your life.

September 23—*The Power of Words*

Your words are very powerful. Your words can work wonders.

Words are magical. Words have power. Words can change any feeling or experience. Words can change your life.

September 24—*It Takes Time*

Getting what you want often takes time. It's a process.

While your goal is in the process of manifesting, you're probably tweaking and fine-tuning it to make it better, getting things just right, polishing and perfecting exactly what you want, and working with the changes as they show themselves.

Take the time your goal requires to manifest in just the way you want it to—to make it perfect and exactly the way you want it to be.

September 25—*Threads*

When you're working on manifesting something in your life—creating your new reality—you'll often find that other things you've previously had on your mind come into being, even things you no longer think about or haven't thought of for a while will appear in your life.

This is because the energy surrounding your desire to manifest something touches and connects with similar energies, threading together related thoughts and energies, gaining even more strength, and before you know it, you've gotten what you wanted and so much more.

September 26—*That's Not What I Expected*

You may not always get what you want; sometimes you get something you weren't expecting. This can be a good thing or a bad thing.

If you have a sense of humor, it makes things easier to accept and gives you a good handle on where they came from. And sometimes you get something better than you expected.

September 27—*Higher Help*

Ask the Universe to help you, especially if you feel stuck. A simple, sincere request can go a long way.

Let yourself receive help from unexpected sources. This help can appear in many ways—a suggestion from someone or a thought that pops into your mind, or something that just seems to happen for no apparent reason which gives you exactly what you need at this particular time.

September 28—*Twists and Turns*

On the way to arriving at the new reality you're creating for yourself, you're going to find many twists and turns along the way.

Twists in the form of delightful surprises and turns where you're going to have to make new choices that will alter the course of your destiny—to see where you've been, how you've gotten to where you are now, and how you need to change course.

The scenery along the way will also change. New opportunities arise, new people and situations will come into your life to help you along the way that you never expected.

September 29—*There's Plenty More Where That Came From*

There is an abundant, never-ending, ever-growing, always replenishing, infinite supply of energy you can tap into at any time you want to or need to.

September 30—*Designs*

Don't you just love it when everything falls into place? When everything works out perfectly?

You created the blueprint and design for this to happen.

October

Choices and Changes

October

Choices and Changes

October 1—**Actions**

It's better to act a new way of thinking, than to think a new way of acting.

October 2—**Blowing in the Breeze**

Let go of everything that doesn't serve you well. Give it to the wind, and let the light, airy breeze blow it away. Let the wind dissipate and carry it away. You feel free and light, happy and carefree.

October 3—**Do Things the Right Way**

There's no right or wrong way to do things. Whatever works for you is the right way. No one ever made up a rule book that works for everyone. But there is one thing that always works the right way—a positive attitude.

You can still accomplish what you want by going about it the wrong way, by worrying about it, wondering when—if ever—it will occur by putting doubtful thoughts about it in your mind. When you go about it this way, it will take a very long time to get what you want and the process will be abjectly miserable; it will be negative and totally unenjoyable.

By putting positive thoughts into your mind, you will find the right way to do things that works for you. Things that will bring you happiness and joy along the way.

October 4—*Change of Plans*

If something isn't working the way you wanted it to or hoped it would, perhaps it's time for a change of plans—a fresh start.

When something isn't working, it's because something better, new, and wonderful is about to happen. Let yourself be open to new ideas and seeing a different direction.

October 5—*Set in Stone*

If something in your life appears to be unchangeable, as if it is set into stone, no matter how hard you try to change it or how much positive energy you put into it, look into why it is happening.

Understand it, know why it's in your life and what it is showing you. Then, take that information and begin to chisel away at the seemingly solid stone.

October 6—*Fear is a Friend*

Fear is a friend who is hidden for the moment.

Turn your fears around; allow them to work for you rather than against you. Accept your fear as a beautiful opportunity or challenge to know yourself better. Acknowledge it as a wonderful chance for inner growth and positive change.

Fear as an enemy will hold you back. Fear as a friend will guide you lovingly and in a supportive manner as you move forward. It's your choice and you're the one with the power to make changes.

October 7—*Change Your Mind*

Change is good. Changing your mind is even better. Changing your mind is wonderful and exhilarating, powerful and scary at the same time. Change inspires you to bigger and better things, and opens many wonderful avenues to explore. Change fills you with energy and invigorates you. You can change anything you want—any thought, feeling, or experience you're having right now. You can tune into your feelings and listen to your inner self—to the knowing within your mind.

You can change your mind and decide to look for the light and joy within yourself. Tuning into the joy and magic within you is as easy as changing your mind. You can change your mind and choose to look for the magical qualities within you.

You can feel the happiness and harmony when you tune into the magical essence within you. You can feel the pure and wonderful joy that is within you—that comes to you simply by looking within yourself and seeing your light.

Change your mind and change your life. Change your mind and decide to look for the light and joy within yourself. Change your life into a joyful expression of the magical essence within you.

October 8—*I'm Gonna Do It!!*

Perhaps you've had a thought running around in your mind for a while about something you're considering doing—something you'd like to do, but for any variety of reasons, you haven't made the commitment to do it. You've been going back and forth between maybe and maybe not whenever you think of doing what it is you're pondering.

Then, suddenly you just know. You get the thought that you CAN do it! You just KNOW you can! And you can do it right now! A feeling of happiness, along with a feeling of great power and energy surges through you. You're actually going to do it!

You wonder what you were waiting for. It all seems so simple and right, like it was always meant to be. You're doing it!

October 9—*Expectations*

You will always get what you expect to get; which is not necessarily what you want. Look into your expectations to see what they show you.

Raise your expectations and beliefs. Work with desire—what you truly want, not what's happened in the past.

Align your expectations with your desires, and follow the flow of that energy.

Look up and forward; not down and back. Feel the joy of what you're creating and know that it will exceed all your expectations.

Change your expectations, and your attitude, to get what you truly want.

October 10—*Should You? Or Shouldn't You?*

If you're wondering whether you *should* do something, or you're not sure about something, or if someone tells you that you "should" do something or "should" do things a certain way, or if you feel you *should* do something—Don't!

The word "should" is a dead give-away that you don't want to do whatever it is you're thinking about. That's why the word "should" comes up in your mind.

You shouldn't do whatever it is you feel you "should" do. Trust your feelings. Trust your inner self. Your inner self knows about these things.

October 11—*How's the Weather?*

I'm sure you've noticed when the weatherman is predicting the weather, he says, "There's a 10% chance of rain." He never says, "There's a 90% chance of sunshine."

In the weather forecast, as well as in your life, you're programmed to look for the negative instead of the positive, even though the positive is all around you.

What if you looked for the sunshine rather than the rain? How would your life be different?

What if you looked for the light within yourself rather than looking at the darkness and shadows all around you?

How would your life be different, filled with light and harmony, happiness and joy?

October 12—*Waffling*

Indecision, not sure about something—whatever you want to call it, you can't make up your mind about something and you're waffling between several choices. Or maybe you want to do something, but not right now. Maybe later, maybe some other time. *Maybe* is telling you that you're not ready to make up your mind.

Put it on hold for a while. Let it simmer in the back of your mind. Think about why you're waffling with *maybe*.

Then, watch what thoughts come to mind to help you make a choice. Listen to your feelings—your intuition—to guide you in the right direction.

October 13—**Hold That Thought**

Hold the thoughts of what you want to happen in your life in your mind and feelings. Think about them every day in a positive way.

But don't hold on too tightly. Let them breathe. Let the vision of what you want float gently through your mind and feelings, gathering the energy they need to manifest.

Hold lightly to your thoughts. Give them room to grow and expand. Give it time for the Universe to step in and create something even better than you first imagined or envisioned.

October 14—**That's So Sad**

There are times in your life when you feel sad about something; perhaps something that has happened to you or something you've seen or been affected by

When you're feeling sad, accept it and embrace it. Let it wash through you. Feeling sad is a natural part of life. Accept it, then let it go.

October 15—**Stepping Stones**

What you perhaps perceive as stumbling blocks are really stepping stones in disguise.

October 16—*Face Your Fears*

If you're afraid of something, perhaps that you'll never achieve a certain goal, face that fear directly.

It exists in your mind so have a conversation with it. Let the fear explain itself to you, so you know where it's coming from and can understand it.

Then work through that fear. It's not real; it's only an imaginary feeling that isn't there anymore because you've understood it.

October 17—*Your Wish is my Command*

Imagine you have a magic lamp, complete with a powerful genie that rises through an ethereal, luminous mist, who can grant your every wish.

This powerful genie resides within your mind. The powerful genie is you. You have the power to grant yourself anything you wish.

Look inside your mind for this magical, powerful genie who is ready to appear and grant you anything and everything your heart desires.

October 18—*Everything is Changeable*

Everything—no matter what it is—is changeable.

October 19—*Cancel, Cancel*

If a negative thought comes to mind, or if you're worried about something, say the words, "Cancel. Cancel." Repeat as necessary.

You don't want a negative thought or worry to take hold in your mind and put down roots.

Negative thoughts and/or worries don't belong in your beautiful mind. Cancel them out.

October 20—*Focus Your Energies*

Wherever you focus your energies, and whatever you focus your energies on, you will draw similar energies to you.

If you focus on the positive, then positive energies which are on a similar vibration to your thoughts will flow to you.

October 21—*Early Warning System*

You have a built-in early warning system that alerts you when you're about to do something wrong. You can feel it inside you as an uh-oh feeling or an uneasy feeling not to do something. It's your inner self telling you not to do something that goes against your better judgment.

This radar—your early warning system—also alerts you when something bad is about to happen or when things are about to go south. You get a bad feeling, a hunch, a premonition, or something doesn't feel quite right. It's your intuition giving you an early warning sign to be on the lookout.

These feelings may be small at first, but pay attention to them. Your magical mind always has your best interests at heart and will warn you when you need it.

October 22—*What's the Best That Could Happen?*

Really think about that for a while. What is the very best thing that could happen to you right now?

October 23—*Previews*

Watch your dreams. They'll accurately portray events to come. Look into your magical mind for previews of coming attractions, shown to you in glorious technicolor.

October 24—*Patterns*

Notice the way you go about doing things. See if there's a pattern—a repetitive action that occurs on a daily, or an almost-daily basis. Or you might want to call this pattern a habit or a routine.

This pattern/habit/routine is a blueprint for what you experience every day. If the pattern is working—if it serves you well, keep it. If it isn't working—if it drains you, change it.

October 25—*It's Scary*

Starting a new goal, or a different way of doing things is scary and exhilarating at the same time.

Maybe you're not sure of the steps you need to take because you're traveling through unfamiliar, uncharted territory and you don't know what to expect or what will happen.

Yes, it can be scary, but it can also be wonderful and joyful, full of unexpected surprises and happy occurrences as you explore new experiences.

Take scary by the hand and bravely walk toward your new reality. It'll be fun; I promise.

You'll be exploring things you've never done before. You'll be learning lots of new things on the way and you'll discover that it's not scary at all. It's fun. It's exciting to travel a new path.

October 26—*Heart and Soul*

When you accomplish something, is it because you put your whole heart and soul into it?

Or did you accomplish it through blood, sweat, and tears?

It's always your choice of how to go about things.

Putting your whole heart and soul into something is the easy way. Everything comes to you naturally.

Blood, sweat, and tears is the hard way and drains your energy. You have to fight for everything that comes your way.

Which way do you want to follow?

October 27—*Traveling Your Path*

There are many paths that lead to the same end goal. There are many ways to achieve what you want. The path you follow will be unique to you. Maybe others have traveled the same path, but in a slightly different direction because they're following their journey which will take them where they want to go.

No one can give you exact directions of how to achieve your goal. Your path, while perhaps following some of the same steps that others have traveled before, will veer off in new directions that will lead you, and guide you perfectly to what you want.

Follow your own path.

October 28—*Try it Again*

If something didn't work out for you the way you wanted it to, try again. Perhaps you need to follow a new direction or perhaps the way before wasn't clear, or you had doubts that tripped you up and blocked your way.

Perhaps the doubts you had can show you that there is a better way to do things. Doubt can show you the way to make things happen by flipping doubt around and seeing the up side.

Your first attempt provided you with a lot of information and insights you can use to guide your way this time.

October 29—*What if...?*

Play with the "what if…" thought and see what happens. Or play with the "what would happen if…" thought.

The "what if" thought creates scenarios in your mind you can play with to see what outcomes might happen, or how you might go about achieving something you want or seeing how it comes to you.

You might also see a new way of doing things, or a new path may unfold before you that will lead you in an entirely different direction to help you achieve what you want, or show you how to go about getting it.

What if your life was everything you want it to be, right here, right now?

October 30—*Know Your Limits*

There's all this talk about letting go of limits and setting yourself free, which is totally the right thing to do in most circumstances.

But limits can be a good thing, especially when you're in the process of creating something you want.

Setting limits allows you to work within a well-defined parameter of what you need to do to bring about what you want, and gives the Universe a clear picture of how to help you.

If you don't set limits, you'll be scattering the energies instead of grouping them together to help you get what you want.

October 31—**Let's Pretend**

Pretend to be someone you want to be, someone who has everything you want. Play the part. Act the part. Feel the part. Dress the part. Be the part. Act as if the part is real.

Pretty soon you're not pretending any more.

November

Gratitude

November

Gratitude

November 1—**Attitude of Gratitude**

Having an "Attitude of Gratitude" offers you a way to fully embrace gratitude in your life and send it forth to everyone around you—to the world, to the universe, and to yourself.

Look within your thoughts and feelings to see how gratitude can open your heart, mind, and soul to all the good that is all around you, everywhere, every day, all the time.

Take a moment—today, and every day—to go quietly within yourself and meditate on what you are grateful for in your life.

When you're done meditating on what you are thankful for, send your feelings of gratitude to everyone and everything around you, and into the Universe. By doing this, you send and receive gratitude for yourself from many sources.

By simply living, breathing, and being with an attitude of gratitude, you can change your life profoundly. Being grateful is a truly amazing gift that brings you so many magical things.

November 2—**The Journey**

If you've set long-time goals for yourself, ones that will take some time to come into full fruition, look at how far you've come;

not how far you have to go. Take some time to appreciate what you've accomplished so far, then set your sights on what you will be achieving in the future.

Then, one step in front of the other and you'll get there. Enjoy the journey.

November 3—*Minor Miracles*

Major, life-changing miracles are wonderful and happen once or twice in a lifetime, maybe even more than a few times.

But minor miracles—the ones that happen every day—the little things that make your life better—are just as wonderful and magnificent as the once-or-twice-in-a-lifetime miracles.

November 4—*Blessings*

Being thankful for everything in your life also means being thankful for what is coming into your life and recognizing the many blessings you already have.

November 5—*Healthy Thoughts*

Take some time to really appreciate the perfect health you have. Too often, you may take your perfect health for granted. Thank your body for taking such good care of you.

If you're experiencing a health concern, look into it to see what thoughts may have precipitated it. See what it has to offer you, and ask your body what you can do to bring about a healing. It might just be your body's way of asking for help.

See what you can do to heal yourself. You may also want to remind yourself that you are perfectly healthy.

November 6—*This is So Awesome!*

As you work toward your goal, take some time along the way to admire and appreciate the work you've accomplished so far, and to see how truly awesome it is.

November 7—*It's too Easy*

If something comes to you easily and you think to yourself that it's too easy, I don't really know how it happened; or what did I do to deserve this wonderful thing, it's because you've already done the work and created the pathway for what's too easy to come into your life. Good job!

November 8—*Time Frame*

Set a time frame in which your new reality will emerge. Setting a time frame motivates you to complete your desired goal and to put forth the necessary energy for it to manifest.

Setting a time frame also allows the Universe to match your energies and bring about the things you want.

Be reasonable and realistic in what you can achieve in a given amount of time, and allow for interesting and beneficial things to happen along the way which you haven't put into the picture.

November 9—*Everything is Going Really Well*

When everything is going really well, be sure to acknowledge that. Thank it and be grateful. Also acknowledge that you're doing everything the right way because everything is going so well.

Keep up the good work.

November 10—*You Can Do Whatever You Want to Do*

You have the power within you to create anything you want—whenever you want it.

Feel the power you have inside you.

November 11—*Admiration*

Admiration is a form of gratitude. When you admire something that someone has done, you send good vibes.

When you admire something you've done, you grow the gratitude.

November 12—***Think About It***

Write down at least thirty things you are grateful for.

Your list can include simple things—maybe things you take for granted—like the warmth of the sun, a nice home to live in, a car to drive, a good job, food in the fridge, as well as major things like a loving relationship or a beloved pet.

Think about how you've brought all these wonderful things into your life and how much they mean to you.

Thank them for being in your life.

November 13—***It's the Little Things***

Little things—that maybe you don't pay much attention to—are often the most important things.

Little things you might take for granted which go unnoticed because they're always there and they've been in your life for a long time.

It's the little things that are perhaps the most important things. Really notice the little things and be grateful they are in your life.

November 14—***I'm Having so Much Fun***

Whatever you're doing, or trying to accomplish, enjoy the process along the way. Notice how much fun you're having.

November 15—***Set a True Course***

What do you need to do that will get you where you want to go? Set a course and follow your own direction.

November 16—***Own it. It's Yours***

Whatever you're experiencing in your life right now has been caused and created by you. It's yours. It belongs to you. Own it. You created it. All of it. Down to the last detail.

If it's good, then take pride in how well you've done. If it's not good, it still belongs to you, as much as you don't want it to. And because it's yours, you have the power to change it into something good you're proud to call your own.

November 17—**Thank You**

Two little words that can make a world of difference. Say "thank you" more often. Several times a day is good. A dozen or more is even better.

November 18—**Count Your Blessings**

Look at all the good in your life. Look at all your blessings. As you count your many blessings, you'll see all the wonderful things you've created and brought into your life. You'll see how you have been blessed in so many ways.

Acknowledge your blessings and embrace all these wonderful things you have.

November 19—**Pay Attention**

Notice the small things. Small things are equally as powerful as the big things, maybe even more so.

Appreciate all the seemingly small things. They're really important because they create the big things.

Notice something in your life that appears small. Take the time to appreciate it and you'll see how powerful and big it truly is.

November 20—**Glimpses**

From who you are now, and where you are in your life right now, look into the past to see where you've been and what you've accomplished and drawn into your life, and how your earlier thoughts and choices have turned out.

Then take a look into the future to see where you're going, what things will be coming to you, and what awaits you. See how the thoughts and choices you make today will turn out in the future.

Plot a course and draw a map to guide you to where you want to go.

November 21—*Goals*

Long-term goals, set to happen in the future, offer promises of many wonderful things to come that will be happening in your life. Set a long-term goal, something that is very special to you. Begin to take the steps that will provide the way for you to achieve it.

Be sure to acknowledge your accomplishments along the way, and be grateful for everything you've achieved so far as you look forward to what's to come that is in line with your goals.

November 22—*Be Reasonable*

Look at what you want to achieve in a reasonable, realistic light. You know what you want and what you are capable of. You know what you can do.

Set realistic goals—ones you know you can achieve. Ones you believe are achievable. But don't be surprised when the Universe steps in and helps you along the way.

November 23—*Acknowledge a Change of Mind*

You can always change your mind if something isn't going the way you want it to. Sometimes changing your mind is the best thing to do—to go in a new direction with fresh thoughts and ideas.

When you change your mind, be sure to acknowledge you've changed your mind. Let your inner self / Universe know that you've changed your mind about something and are now moving in a different direction. Otherwise, your inner self / Universe will continue to try to create what you originally envisioned.

November 24—*Being Thankful*

Be thankful for everything in your life—the good, the bad, the ugly, and the beautiful. It's all part of you. Everything serves a wonderful purpose and helps you become the magical person you truly are.

Be thankful for everything that happens to you. See the good in it and how it has helped you to grow.

November 25—*What's the Rush?*

Sometimes it's hard to wait for what you see in your mind to manifest on a physical level.

You can see it; you believe it; you've been working toward it; you know it's going to happen—but when will it ever come into your life?

Some things take time. Time moves much slower on a physical level than on the magical level inside your mind. Time, in the atmosphere of creation, doesn't follow the same rules as time, as you know it, on a physical level.

Keep the faith. Keep the picture in your mind. It's already happening and will appear in your life at the right time.

November 26—*I Give Up*

This doesn't mean what you think it might at first.

Give up your request and desire for something to occur to the Universe and let the positive energies you've created gather even more energy to manifest what you want.

Let go; give it up, and let the Universe help you.

November 27—*It's Done!*

See your goal as already accomplished. Even though it may be in the beginning stages, seeing it as a completed project will cause energies to come into play that will actually bring about your goal.

Notice how you feel about accomplishing something you truly wanted. Be appreciative and thankful for all you've accomplished. Feel the gratitude you'll feel when your goal is accomplished.

Hold on to that feeling while your goal is in the process of being accomplished.

November 28—*Gaining Momentum*

Immerse yourself in the energy of whatever it is you're creating for yourself. As your new reality—the one you want; the one you've envisioned—begins to appear in your life, it gathers strength and momentum, and seems to grow of its own accord and takes off full speed ahead as it takes you along for the ride.

November 29—*It's No Bother*

If something is bothering you, do something about it. Don't let it bother you. Fix whatever it is so it no longer bothers you. Look into it and understand it. Why are you bothered by whatever it is?

The "bother" doesn't want to be there; it doesn't want to bother you. The bother will show you exactly what to do to "un-bother" it.

Follow your feelings and listen to your insights to find a way to un-bother it.

November 30—*It's a Date*

Set a specific date in which you want something to manifest. Give it enough time to grow, develop, and come into being. Stick to your schedule of things you need to do and do what needs to be done—on your part—to make your new reality happen on a specific date.

The Universe will match your energy and intention. But give yourself some leeway and be prepared for changes along the way. Other things may have to happen in order for your goal to manifest. Put in some extra time in your schedule to allow for positive changes to occur.

December

Giving and Receiving

December

~

Giving and Receiving

December 1—**Ripples**

Everything you say and do has a ripple effect, touching and affecting everyone you know, even everyone you don't know.

It's like throwing a pebble in a pond—the concentric circles ripple ever-outward, touching and affecting all the water in the pond.

Your ripple effect is far-reaching. It may even come back and touch you one day.

Make good ripples—the kind you'd like to receive.

December 2—**The Present is a Gift**

While it's important to look forward—to see what you want and to set goals, the present is the real gift.

The present is where and how you create your future. The present is where your real power is. Treasure the gift of the present.

What are you doing right now in this present moment?

December 3—**Options**

Make room for special surprises to happen. Allow something even better to occur than what you had originally envisioned.

December 4—*Brighten Up Your Day*

You look really nice today!

Did that make you smile? Did you feel happy because someone paid you a compliment? Did it brighten your day and lift your spirits?

You really do look nice today.

That's a very generic compliment, but even something as general as that can work wonders. A compliment, sincerely given, will brighten up your day and the day of the person receiving it.

Today, take the time to really notice something special about someone—it can be a stranger or a friend—and compliment them on it.

December 5—*Ready, Willing, and Able*

The Universe is ready, willing, and able to give you anything and everything you can imagine.

The Universe is filled with infinite energy and power, and will give you more than you can ever want or need.

Whatever you want is yours for the asking.

December 6—*Focus Your Energies*

You probably have a lot of stuff going on.

There's this thing you want to do. Then, there's that thing you also want to do. There's the other thing, too.

And there's probably lots of other stuff, in the form of distractions, vying for your attention.

Focus your energies. If you try to focus on too many things at once, you'll dissipate the energy. Stay focused on what is important to you right now. Prioritize what you really want to do.

For the distractions, which are usually minor little things, direct your attention to the things that need to be done, do them, and be done with them, then return your focus to the wonderful reality you're creating for yourself.

December 7—*Receiving*

Allow yourself to receive all the good in your life. It's simple and easy.

Just allow yourself to be open to receiving all the wonderful things that flow into your life. Acknowledge that you accept all the good you have and all the good to come.

December 8—*For Goodness Sake*

You have so much goodness inside you. You are overflowing with an always-replenishing supply of goodness. Let all the good come out.

December 9—*Power Positives*

Here are a few words and phrases you might like to incorporate into your vocabulary every day. Some of these may sound like hyperbole, but they really work and make a huge difference in how you see and feel about things.

Wow! It's perfect! Wonderful! Special! This is really working! I'm so happy! Thank you! Totally awesome! Yay! That's so nice! Beautiful! This is so much fun! Good job!

YAY!! Works best when combined with simultaneous hand clapping, and jumping up and down with sheer joy. A happy dance has also been known to occur.

I'm so happy! This is usually accompanied by uncontrollable laughter and absolute joy.

Perfect likes to be repeated several times, at least three times in a row, getting louder each time. Perfect! *Perfect!* **PERFECT!**

This is so much fun! Usually said with a giggle in your voice and accompanied by a few bounces and an eagerness to do more of what's so fun.

This is really working! This works in combination with feelings of awe, an intake of breath or a gasp of amazement, a great, big wide smile, and an unconscious bringing up of both hands to your heart.

That's so nice works much, much better when the word "so" is emphasized, when it's pronounced louder and drawn out longer than the other words.

These are just a few suggestions for words you might want to say on a daily basis.

December 10—*Pleasant Surprises*

Don't be surprised when the Universe gives you things you never asked for or expected. These gifts are the way the Universe shows you that you're on the right track and rewards your efforts.

There are so many fringe benefits when you create the reality you want from a good place in your heart and mind.

December 11—*It's a Deal*

Hey, Universe... Here's the deal.

I'll do "this" if you do "that" but you have to do "that" before I'll do "this."

Umm, no. Doesn't work that way, no matter how nicely you ask.

You have to do "this" before "that" will happen.

December 12—*The Gift of Giving*

What do you have to give? What can you "gift" someone with today?

The gift can be monetary, like buying someone a cup of coffee, or it can come from your heart, like a smile you give a stranger or a hug you give to a friend.

Notice how their eyes light up and a big smile comes to their face. Notice how your heart feels happier and lighter.

And be sure to notice how much better and brighter you feel inside. You've touched their spirit with light, and they, in return, with their response, have touched your spirit.

What gifts do you have to share? When you give of yourself, it's a gift that keeps on giving.

Who knows how far the coffee will warm someone? Who knows how far your smile will travel? Who knows how much the gentle touch on someone's shoulder or the hug will be felt?

December 13—*Are You Ready?*

Are you ready to accept your new reality?

It's going to happen. Your new reality—the one you've been creating based on what you want—is making its way to you.

Get ready and be prepared to accept and love your new reality.

December 14—*Try Something Different*

There's something you've been wanting to do. Something new and different that appeals to you, that creates a sense of excitement within you.

Let yourself experience this new and wonderful thing.

December 15—*Let it Go*

When you reach a certain point in creating your reality—when you've built the foundation and structured the framework—let it go and let the Universe do the rest.

Continue to feed your desired reality with focus and attention, but it's out of your hands now—it's already in the process of manifesting.

December 16—*Gifting*

What can you "gift" yourself with today? It can be something tangible or intangible.

What is a gift you want more than anything?

December 17—*Making Mistakes*

There's no such thing as a mistake. There are only positive learning experiences—learning to do something differently to achieve what you want. Let these "seeming" mistakes show you a new way of doing things.

December 18—*Trusting*

Trust that the things you want and need will always be there for you. You don't need to know how they will come about; you just need to know they will always be there when you need them.

December 19—*Kindness Counts*

A kind act, a kind gesture, a kind comment matters so much more than you may think it does.

A simple act of kindness can work wonders in someone's life, perhaps even turning it around.

Give kindness whenever and wherever you can.

December 20—*Acceptance*

Accepting things as they are in your life right now is the first step to creating what can be.

Acknowledge that you created them in the first place and allowed them into your life, then see how you want to change them.

See things for what they are to show you how you want to change them and why you want to change them—how you want to grow them into an experience you'd really like to have in your life.

December 21—*Uplifting*

Have you ever noticed, when you were in a dark place filled with sadness and despair, that there was something—perhaps a feeling or a thought, or you sensed a presence—that lifted you up out of that place?

That was your inner self (you may also want to call it your higher self, or your guardian angel, or your spirit, or the Universe) lifting you up out of despair and filling you with light.

December 22—*Promises*

Make a promise—a sacred vow—to yourself about something that's really important and special to you.

Keep that promise.

December 23—*Appreciation*

Show appreciation for something nice someone has done for you. Show appreciation for something nice you've done for someone else.

Show appreciation for something nice that happened to you. Show appreciation for something nice you did for yourself.

December 24—*The Best Present—Ever!*

If you could have anything you wanted, what would that be?

How can you go about "gifting" yourself with what you truly want?

You have the power and an amazing gift of creating your reality—of allowing everything you could ever want to be in your life.

Use your power and "gift" yourself with something very special—something you've always wanted.

December 25—*A Gift From the Universe*

You hear a soft, whooshing sound above you as a white gift box tied with a purple ribbon gently falls from the sky, landing softly beside you.

Picking it up, knowing it's a gift from the Universe, you open it and see what's inside.

December 26—*The End is Here*

No, not that end with the tunnel and white light and a beautiful angel.

The end of the journey of reaching your goal has arrived. You've put forth a tremendous amount of positive energy toward reaching your goal and now you've accomplished it. Well done!

Your inner self, who has been with you all along, championing your every step along the way is jumping for joy at your achievement and the Universe is smiling at you, showering you with light, reaching out to touch your soul.

Take a deep breath and feel the joy in your accomplishment.

But you know what this means, don't you? There's a new beginning just waiting to happen—to grow into your new best thing.

December 27—Celebrate

When you accomplish something—whether it's big or small—have a celebration to honor what you've achieved.

Announce your accomplishment. Share it with friends and family, and with the world, if appropriate.

You did it! You are awesome!

December 28—Give Freely

If someone needs your help, give it freely, without expecting anything in return. Give it just because someone needs your help. Give it because you want to help someone, and because it makes you feel good.

If you do something nice for someone, do it freely, without expecting a favor or anything else in return. Do something nice just for the sake of doing something nice.

When you give freely, you give sincerely from your heart. Then, whatever you give is truly a gift.

When you do this, the Universe will notice and reward you for your kindness. But don't expect the Universe to do this. It will only happen if you give freely.

December 29—Follow-Through

When you say you're going to do something, it's important to follow-through on what you say you're going to do.

You're directing positive energies toward doing what you say.

December 30—It's All Yours

You can have everything you want. The Universe wants you to have whatever you want.

December 31—**Reflections**

Look back at this past year before you look forward to the next year. Reflect on this past year to see the beautiful mind garden you've planted and nurtured with care and love.

See how you've grown your mind into a magical mind garden, filled with harmony and joy, happiness and light.

About the Author

Thanks for reading this book. I hope you've enjoyed growing your mind into a magical mind garden of harmony and joy.

Gloria Chadwick writes an eclectic mix of books—from angels to Zen. Her nonfiction books cover positive mind power, meditation, past lives, and journeys in heaven. Her novels cover time travel adventures in parallel worlds, metaphysical mysteries, and cozy fantasy adventures into magical worlds. She's also written a few cookbooks and some lighthearted guides for writers.

Please visit **Morpheus Books** to browse her books—https://morpheusbooks.blogspot.com.

Magical Mind, Magical Life

Your mind is magical. You are magical.
You hold the key to a magical life within your mind.

This book is an adventuresome, interactive guide into opening the magical power inside your mind.

It offers you a journey of self-discovery and shows you how to create miracles in every moment by using the magical power of your mind to enjoy a happier, more fulfilled life.

You can make your life everything you want it to be and more. You have this power within you now; it's not something new or something you have to learn.

All you have to do is look within yourself—look within the power of your own mind and put that magic to work for you.

This life-changing book invites you to open, explore, experience, and understand the natural power of your mind. It's a guide that shows you the way to living a magical life, filled with happiness and light.

Inner Journeys

Guided visualizations can take you on many wonderful inner journeys that lead you into the multidimensional worlds of your mind and soul.

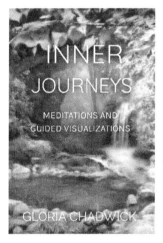

Inside this book you'll find metaphysical, magical, mystical meditations that will inspire and empower you on your path of self-discovery and spiritual awareness.

They're offered to illuminate and guide your way as you travel an inner journey into yourself, into rediscovering your spiritual knowledge and reuniting with your higher self.

In addition, meditating offers you many practical benefits, including a refreshing, rejuvenating break from your day-to-day activities; clarity, calmness, and peace of mind; a quiet, tranquil time to tune into your inner self; a wonderful sense of relaxation and well-being; and health and harmony within your body, mind, and spirit.

Made in United States
North Haven, CT
15 June 2024